Chautauqua Springs, Kansas, 1888

The names of places of interest, stores, store owners, shoppers,

And visitors

Chautauqua Springs, Kansas

Jan. 15, 2017 The Advertiser Journal (Sedan, Kansas)
12-24-1936-2-25-1937

A black eagle was killed near Hewins. Floyd Blankenship of Hewins was in Sedan displaying a large black eagle he killed near Hewins. Thinking the bird was a hawk he took a shot at it killing it. The eagle had a wing spread of five and one half feet.

1-14-37

A new meat market opens: A. J. Floyd and son Darrel Saturday opened a Grocery and Market in the Floyd building on Main Street, formerly occupied by the Frank Harmon Grocery.
Mr. Floyd formerly was in the grocery business in Sedan and is the Ordering County Commissioner from District 2. For the past two years Darrel has worked as Government Meat Inspector and later in a large meat market in Kansas City and has much experience in that line. Mr. and Mrs. Darrel Floyd have moved from Kansas City to Sedan.

Floyds Market-Groceries and Meats

Oranges-Sunkist-each 1c
Coffee-fresh roasted and ground 15c pd.
Beans No. 2 can 9c
Sugar, cloth bag 10 pds 54c
These prices are for Saturday only
Pork Neck Bones 2 pds 15c
Fresh Beef Brains 2 pds 15c
Short Cut Steaks 1 pd 12.5c
Pork Roast Shoulder Cuts 1 pd. 14.5c
Pork Steak 1 pd 18.5c
Pure Lard 2 pds 29c

Cash and Carry. Pay Cash and Save
Floyds Market, Sedan, Kansas

The Advertiser Journal Vol. 4 No. 37
Sedan, Kansas Feb. 18, 1937

Chautauqua News: Fawna Cooper preached at the Assembly of God Church Friday.

The Chautauqua Express W. J. Wright Editor

May 11, 1888

The Elephant Livery Stable
Clotfelter and Booth proprietors

Good rigs, Good saddle horses furnished at the most reasonable prices.
We run a Daily Hack to and from the Osage Agency, Indian Territory.
A share of your patronage solicited.

Lunch Room- when you want a good dish of ice cream, a good glass of lemonade, or a good Lunch and hot coffee. Go to George Vaughn's Lunch Room.
I also keep constantly on hand a full line of Candies, Nuts, Cigars, Tobaccos, Canned Goods Etc. Don't forget the place ---Third door South of Post Office. Chautauqua Springs, Kansas

Lew Lynn- Justice of the Peace. Legal papers drawn with neatness and dispatch. Office west side Main Street.

Charles Kaufman - Dr. Hass Hog Remedy kept on hand. For anything in my line give me a call. Cigars, Tobaccos, and Pop.

Long Bell Lumber Company

Lumber, Lath, Shingles, Sash, Doors, Lime, Moulding, Cement, Hair, and Paints.
We also carry a full line of Hardware, Stoves, Tin ware, and Barbwire.

For anything in our line give us a call before buying elsewhere.
W. A. Franks, Manager.

Millinery Goods

At Mrs. Mary Lee's. Hats, Ribbons, Plushes, Velvets, Trimmings and everything usually kept in a first class Millinery. Call on me. South end Main Street, Chautauqua. Call on me Mrs. M. Lee.

Furniture and Undertaker
T. J. Johnson, proprietor

I Have just received a large and well selected stock of Furniture consisting of Chairs, Safes, Bedsteads, Stands, Tables, Mattresses, At which I will sell at the lowest cash price. Call on me.

Col. Howard will stand for the season of 1888 at the Elephant Livery Stable. Col. Howard is 9 years old this spring and 16 hands high, a beautiful sorrel and a perfect model horse. He has never lost a premium in his class has showed over the Night Of Saint Louis at Liberty, Plattsburg, Platts City, Pleasant Hill, Harrisonville, and Kansas City of Saint Lois and other celebrated horses. Terms- $5.00 for a single leap, $10.00 for the season, $20.00 to insure mare with colt, $15.00 will be charged to insure colt.

Methodist Episcopal Church, Reverend W. S. Browning pastor Services Sunday Morning at 11:00 and 8 p.m. on first and third Sabbath at 8:00. Services beginning promptly. Converts meeting at the parsonage every Thursday evening.

Union Sunday School   Reverend: C. W. Caldwell
Pastor Services every Sunday at 11 am and 8 pm every second and third Sunday. Convert meeting at the parsonage every Thursday evening.

J. Jacks last week brought in 5 small coyotes less than a week old to be distributed among those in want of such pets.

Monroe and Company dealers in Staples and Fancy Groceries, canned goods, Provisions : Flour, Graham, Cigars, Tobacco's, Pop, and Cold Lunch, Country Produce, taken in exchange for goods at high prices. East Side Main Street, Chautauqua, Kansas

J. B. Beaston City Auctioneer will cry any sales in the city or country.

Office on Main Street Chautauqua Springs.

C. C. Purcell Notary Public.

Purcell and Beaston   Real Estate and Exchange Agents

Farms, Raw Lands, and Stock Ranches for sale or trade.
Merchandise to exchange for lands

Chautauqua Springs, Kansas

C. C. Purcell's Broker Office!

Money to loan on Personal or Chattel Security on 30, 60, 0r 90 days.

Deeds, Mortgages, Bills of Sale and all other legal instruments drawn with neatness. Insurance Broker, Collection Agent, and Notary Public. Office on Main Street, Chautauqua, Kansas.

J. N. Goff Dealer in Harness, Saddles, Bridles, Whips, Collars,

Robes, Brushes, Combs, and in fact everything usually kept in a first class Harness Shop. Repairing neatly done.

B. F. Barrett   Boots and Shoes
I have the best assortment of boots and shoes in Southern Kansas Which I am selling at Bed Rock Prices for Spot Cash. Come and inspect my stock.

May 18, 1888 The Chautauqua Express W. J. Wright Editor

Methodist Episcopal Church Reverend W. S. Browning

Pastor. Services every Sunday am at 11 am and at 8 pm every second and forth week of the month. Convert meeting at the parsonage every Thursday evening.

Union Sunday School meets every Sabbath morning at 10:00. Parents bring your children.

Chautauqua G. A. R. Post No 218 Meets every Saturday on or before the full moon of each month and every two weeks thereafter. J. W. Sipple and Agent J. B. Stallard.

The King of Spain is 18 months old and gets 18 million dollars

Europe used $65,000,000.00 worth of pork in spite of the efforts to exclude? The American hog might not be absolutely perfect but the Old World cannot get along without him.

Charles Kaufman – Cigars, Tobaccos, and Pop. Also carries Dr. Haas Hog Remedy. For anything in my line give me a call.

Long Bell Lumber Company carries Lumber, Lath, Shingles, Sash, Doors, Lime, Moulding, Cement, Hair, and Paint. We also carry a full line of Hardware, Stoves, Tin-ware, and Barbwire. For anything in our line give us a call before buying elsewhere. W. A. Frank Manager.

Millinery Goods at Mrs. Mary Lees. Hats, Ribbons, Plushes, Velvets, Trimmings, and everything usually kept in a first class Millinery Store. South end Main Street, Chautauqua, Mrs. M. Lee

Furniture and Undertaker T. J. Johnson Proprietor. I have just received a large well selected stock of furniture consisting of Chairs, Sofas, Bedsteads, Stands, Tables, Mattresses, which I will sell at the lowest Cash prices. Call and see me.

Col. Howard will stand for a season of 1888 at the Elephant Livery Stable. Description: Col Howard is 9 years old this spring, 16 hands high, a beautiful sorrel and a perfect horse. Has never lost a premium in his class and has been showed at Liberty, Pittsburg, Platte City, Pleasant Hill. Harrisonville, and Kansas

City Mo. and took premium over the Knight of Saint Louis and other celebrated horses. A good pasture with plenty of grass and water will be furnished mare from distance free of charge. Col. Howard is a Thoroughbred registered horse. P. R. Raines

Sipple and Pershall are dealers in Dry Goods, Clothing, Boots, Shoes, Hose, Underwear, Notions, Fancy Groceries and Provisions which are selling at the lowest living prices we keep in stock a full line of Drugs, Medicines, Chemicals, and Oils, Prescriptions carefully compounded. New fresh goods constantly arriving. You are invited to come and inspect our stock and get our prices. Sipple and Pershall. Chautauqua, Kansas.

Lew Lynn   Notary Public and Justice of the Peace
Legal Papers drawn up with neatness and dispatch. Office West side of Main Street.

Monroe and Company   dealer in Staple and Fancy Groceries. Canned   goods and provisions, Flour, Graham, Cigars, Tobaccos, Pop and Cold Lunch. Country Produce taken in exchange for goods at highest prices.
East side of Main Street Chautauqua, Kansas.

   C. C. Purcell and Beaston
Real Estate and Exchange Agents. Farms, Raw Lands, and Stock Ranches for sale or trade. Merchandise to exchange for lands. We control the sale of the choicest city property and will sell the same on easy terms. Office on Main Street. Chautauqua Springs, Kansas

Country Lard at Cadwells.

Go to Uncle Jims for a pop

Cadwells for lawns 5c yard

New Drugs at G. L. Dunn and Co.

J. R. Antram, F. Scott was in the city last Monday.

Hailstones were the order of the day last Tuesday.

For a good suit of clothes go to Sipple and Pershalls.

Call at A. C. Cadwell's and see his fine line of silverwares.

P. B. Miller of Kansas City was in town on Monday last.
Mama, buy me a pair of those fine slippers at Barret's.

The editor of the Cedarvale Star was in the city last Saturday.

Wheat is rapidly heading out and harvest is not very far distant.

Alonzo Vancil of the Osage Agency was in the city last Wednesday.

P. R. Rains is acting as City Marshall for the present at any rate.

Jack Quinn accompanied by his son John of oak Valley were in
the city last Friday.

Sipples and Pershall handle the celebrated Kendall boots and
shoes. None can beat them.

George Vaughn and Thos Dunn went down to the Territory
last Monday to look at some cattle.

Reverend W. S. Browning has moved into his commodious
dwelling in the north eastern part of the city,

Topeka has an ice factory which turns out 25 tons per day frozen
from condensed steam.

John Harshburger killed a fine beef last Wednesday. John says
you can now have plenty of fresh meat.

J. S. Frazier who is connected with the Elephant Livery Stable
Made a business trip to Havana last Wednesday.

J. E. Baker treated the front of the building just south of the post
office to a new coat of paint.

Mrs. Nettie Kidd and Mrs. Nettie Green were pleasant callers at the office last Monday. Thanks ladies and call again.

Sipple and Pershall will accept stock of all kinds or notes in payments of accounts or which will exchange goods for stock and notes.

The best washing machine in the world is now for sale at Barretts. You should stop by and see them.

Mrs. M. Rains New York Millinery Store. Please call and examine before purchasing elsewhere. Dressmaking and plain sewing done to order.

Another refreshing shower was a most welcome visitor last Tuesday night. Rain is what makes the corn bloom up but has everlasting done up the cinch bugs.

Mrs. Mary Lee has removed her stock of millinery goods into the Store room formerly occupied by Mr. Bennett as a grocery store where she invites all to call and see her.

Dry apples and peaches at Cadwells.

Ed Grover, owing to a severe swelling on his instep was compelled to resort to the use of crutches this week to enable him to walk. Ed says it is no fun to have to use artificial limbs to walk on.

The ladies of this city are making preparations to present the G. A. R. Post of Chautauqua a handsome new flag. This is a kind act and they will be remembered by the Post for their kindness.

W. W. Franks father of our genial lumberman W. A. Franks left Tuesday morning for McCuen, Kansas where he intends visiting friends a couple of weeks than to Weir City where he will remain till fall.

The Chautauqua Express   W. J. Editor May 25, 1888

City of Chautauqua Springs

Mayor: C. C. Purcell -- Councilmen: Jake Kaufman, J. L. Stallard,
J. B. Dunn, W. E. Mc Guire, A. J. Jacks, F. J. Fritch.
City Clerk W. A. Franks -Treasurer
Chautauqua County Joint Stock Fair Ass. Jack Pershall –Pres.
J. T. Smith --Vice Pres. Lew Lynn – Sec, E.R. Bennet Treasurer,
Jacob Fuller- General Superintendent

Methodist Episcopal Church   W. S. Browning Pastor
Services every first and third Sabbath at 8 p.m. Will begin
Promptly.

U. B. Church   Revered C.W. Alldridge Pastor Services every
Sunday 11am and 8 pm every Thursday evening.

Union Sunday School meets every Sabbath am at 10. Parents
bring your children.

Union Sunday School meets every Sabbath A.M. at 10. Parents bring
your children. W. E. Mc Guire Supt.

Chautauqua G. A. R. Post 218 meets every Sat. on or before the full
moon each month and every two weeks after. J. B. Stallard
J.W. Sipple Capt.

Chosen Friends Lodge 100F
No. 285 Meets every Thurs. evening at their hall
J. F. Smith Hawkins, Recording Secretary.

Man is like a shoe because it is good for the soul to be well heeled.
A man who was troubled with water on the brain claimed it was
caused by a crick in his back.

Advertising is called blowing because it makes full sales, it is called 'puffing' because it swells the profits.

Kansas owes less than any State in the Union and has at present the most healthy prospect for a bountiful crop.

If you are poor there is one consolidation your heirs will not go into court to prove you are an imbecile during your childhood, an idiot at the time of your marriage and a gibbering lunitic for years before you died.

T. J. Dunn and son Physicians and Surgeons offices on west side of Main Street. Also a full line of Drugs and Chemicals for commercial practice.

Commercial Hotel   J. E. Baker Proprietor. First class $1.00 per day. House has good clean beds and rooms and table furnished with the best the market can afford.

C. C. Purcell Brokers Office. Money to loan on Personal or Chattel Security on 30, 60, or 80 days.

Eastern people are bound to look to Kansas this year for a share of it's product to live on.

At the state agriculture college this year there will be on trial some fifty varieties of wheat, 40 of corn, 30 0f sorghum, How does this size up for an institution?

A real estate man at Wichita has managed to fraudulently Mortgage several pieces of property in the city and has found it necessary to at once look up a new location. Detectives have been employed to arrest him but at last accounts nothing was learned Of his whereabouts.

When in Elgin stop and eat at Shinn's Cafe. Prices reasonable Managers Mr. and Mrs. L. J. Ball. (Feb. 1937)

Charles Kaufman—Cigars, Tobaccos, Pop. Dr. Haas' Hog Remedy kept on hand. For any thing in my line give me a call.

Long Bell Lumber Company—Lath, Shingles, Sash, Doors, Lime, Moulding, Cement, Hair, and Paints. We also carry a full line of Hardware, Tin ware, and Barbwire. W.A. Franks , Manager

Millinery Goods at Mrs. Mary Lees –Hats, Ribbons, Plushes, Velvet, Trimmings, and everything usually kept in a first class Millinery Store. Call one me. Mrs. M. Lee. South end Main Street, Chautauqua, Kansas.

Furniture and Undertaker—T.J. Johnson, Proprietor—Chairs, Safes, Bed Steads, Stands, Tables, Mattresses at which I will sell at the Lowest Cash Price. Call and see me.

Col. Howard will stand for season of 1888 at the Elephant Livery Stable. P. R. Raines

T.J. Dunn and Son Physicians and Surgeons- Office on West side of Main Street. Also a full line of Drugs and Chemicals. For Prescription call on us.

Sipple and Pershall- Clothing, Boots, shoes, Hats, Hose, Under Wear, Notions, and so forth. We also carry a full line of staples.

Groceries and Provisions and so forth which we are selling at the lowest living prices. We keep a stock of full line of Drugs, Medicines, Chemicals, Oils, and so forth. Prescriptions carefully Compounded. New, fresh goods constantly arriving. You are invited to come and inspect our stock and get our prices. Sipple and Pershall. Chautauqua, Kansas.

Lew Lynn Notary Public and Justice of the Peace. Legal Papers Drawn with neatness and dispatch. Office west side Main Street. Chautauqua, Kansas

Monroe and Company -- Dealers in Staple and Fancy Groceries, Canned goods, Provisions, Flour, Graham, Cigars, Tobaccos, Pop

and Cold Lunch. Country Produce taken in exchange for goods at the highest prices.
East Side Main St, Chautauqua, Kansas

C. C. Purcell, Notary Public   John B. Beaston, Real Estate
We have a large list of improved Farms, Raw Lands, and Stock Ranches for Sale and Trade. Merchandise to exchange for lands. We control the sale of the choicest city property and will sell the same on easy terms. Office on Main Street, Chautauqua, Springs, Kansas.
We have a large list of improved Farms, Raw Lands, and Stock Ranches for sale or Trade. Merchandise to exchange for lands. We control the sale of the choicest city property and will sell the same on easy terms. Office on Main Street, Chautauqua Springs, Kansas.

Commercial Hotel –J. E. Baker Prop. First class $1.00 per house. Good clean beds and rooms, and tables furnished with the best the market can afford.

J. B. Beaston City Auctioneer. Will cry sales in the city or country. Off Main Street. Chautauqua Springs, Kansas.

Clotfelter and Booth Prop. of The Elephant Livery Stable.
Good rigs, good saddle horses furnished with the most reasonable prices. We run a daily hack to and from the Osage Agency Indian Territory. A share of your Patronage appreciated.

B. F. Barrett—Boots and Shoes – I have the best assortment of Boots and Shoes in Southern Kansas which I am selling at Bed Rock Prices for Spot Cash. Call and inspect my stock.

C. C. Purcell's – Brokers Office—Money to loan on Personal or Chattel Security on 30, 60, or 90 days. Office on Main Street, Chautauqua, Kansas

J. N. Goff- Dealer in Harness, Saddles, Bridles, Whips, Collars, Robes, Brushes, Combs, and in fact everything usually kept in a first class Harness Shop. Repairing neatly don.

Lunch Room—When you want a good dish of Ice Cream, a good glass of lemon Ade, or a good lunch, hot coffee and so forth go to George Vaughn's Lunch Room. I also keep constantly on hand a full line of Candies, Nuts, Cigars, Tobaccos, Canned Goods and so forth. Don't forget the place, third door South of Post Office. Chautauqua, Springs, Kansas

J. E. Baker- dealer in Groceries, Flour, and Provisions. Also a full line of Cigars, Tobaccos, Notions, and everything kept in a good grocery store. Call and get prices before buying elsewhere.

W. E. Mc Guire and A. J. Mc Guire
Mc Guire Brithers

Is the only place where you can get everything you want from a Harvester to a Toothpick.
Dealers in Staple Groceries, Notions, Dry Goods, and so forth.
Hardware
Stoves, Tin ware, Barbwire,
Stock taken in exchange for goods.

W. J. WRIGHT editor   May 25, 1888

City of Chautauqua Springs
 Mayor C. C. Purcell---Councilman—Jake Kaufman, J. L. Stallard, J. B. Dunn, W. E. Mc Guire, A. J. Jacks, F. J. Fritch,--City Clerk W. A. Franks—Treasurer

Chautauqua County Joint Fair Ass. J. T. Pershall-Pres. , J. T. Smith Vice Pres., Lew Lynn Sec.—E. R. Bennet-Treasurer- Jacob Fuller Gen. Supervisor

Methodist Episcopal Church   Rev. W. S. Browning Pastor

U. B. Church   Rev. C. W. Alldredge, Pastor

Union Sunday School W. E. McGuire Supt.

C.Q. G. A. R.   J. B. Stallard--J. W. Supple agent P.C.

Chosen Friends Lodge 100F
No 285 Meets every Thus. eve at their hall
J. F. Smith N.G.
C. C. Purcell, Per. Secy. T. F. Hawkins Re. Secy

R. R. Time Table
Chicago/Kansas and Western Rail Road
Pass. Going East   8:35
Pass. Going West   7:15
Freight going East 1:05
Freight going W   3:55
Freights run East Mon., Wed., and Friday
Freight runs West on Tues., Thurs,, and Sat.

May has it's draw backs- Spring poetry and Housecleaning

The political pot is beginning to boil and the candidates will soon be in hot water.

Kansas has 11 candidates for Governor with several back counties to yet be heard from.

A man who was troubled with water on the brain claimed it was caused by a crick inn his back.

Kansas owes less than any State in the Union and has at present the most healthy looking prospect for a beautiful crop.

If you are poor there is one consolidation, your heirs will not go into court to prove that you were an imbecile during your childhood, an idiot at the time of your marriage and a gibbering lunatic for years before you died.

Charles Kaufman   Cigars, Tobacco, and Pop.

Long Bell Lumber Company—W. A. Frank mgr.

Millinery Goods at
Mary Lee's. South end Main Street, Chautauqua, Kansas

A Furniture and Undertaker—T. J. Johnson Prop.

Col. Howard Standing at Stud Service   P. R. Rains

T. J. Dunn and Son—Physicians and Surgeons
W. side of Main Street. Also a full line of Drugs and Chemicals
For Prescription Practice.

Commercial Hotel—J. E. Baker prop.
First class $1.00 day house. Good clean beds and rooms and table
furnished with the best of Market affords.

C. C. Purcell Broker office. Office on Main Street, Chautauqua, Kan.

The Elephant Livery Stable. Clotfelter and Booth Proprietors.
Osage Agency   Indian Territory

J. B. Beaston—Cit Auctioneer –Office on Main Strret, Chautauqua
Springs, Kansas

Sipple and Pershall—Dry Goods, Clothing, Books, Shoes, Hats,
Hose, Underwear, and Notions. We also carry a full line of Staples
and Fancy Groceries Provisions. We keep a full line of Drugs,
Medicines, Chemicals, Oils, Etc. New fresh goods continually.
Sipple and Pershall, Chautauqua, Kansas.

Lew Lynn- Notary Public and Justice of the Peace. Legal papers
drawn with neatness and dispatch.
Office West side of Main Street. Chautauqua, Kansas

Monroe and Company—Dealers in Staples and Fancy Groceries,
Canned Goods, Provisions, Flour, Graham, Cigars, Tobaccos, Pop,
and Cold Lunch. Country Produce taken in exchange for Goods at
highest prices. East Side Main Street. Chautauqua, Kansas.

C. C. Purcell, Notary Public/Purcell and Beaston
Real Estate and Exchange Agent
Farms, Raw Land, and Stock Ranches for sale or trade. March to exchange for lands. We control the sale of the choicest city properties and will sell the same on easy terms.
Office on Main Street, Chautauqua Springs, Kansas

C. Q. Express 5-25-1888 W.J. Wright

Cadwells for Lawns- 5c a yard
New drugs at G. L. Dunn and Co.
Screne wire at the Lumber yard.
Lawns 4.5c at McGuire Bro.
Screne doors at Long Bell Lumber yard
Mayor Purcell made a bus trip to Independence last Monday.
Straw Hats for men and boys at prices to suit the times at Sipple and Pershall's.

Call at Cadwell's soon to see his Nain socks, linens, Lawns, and prints for they are going fast,
Best baking powder at McGuire Brothers at 15c.
The best washing machine in the world for sale at Barretts
You should stop in and see them. /it will be well worth your while.
Look at those new style screne doors at McGuire Brothers
McGuire Bro. have just received a new lot of white dress goods, lawn, 0rints, muslin, etc. while they are selling for a song

Dr. B. H. Dixon was a pleasant caller at this office last Saturday and had us print him some posters. He has been located at the Eagle Hotel and made dental work a specialty.

Mr. Gilleson, general agent for the Advance Threshing Machine in company with Frank Cross and B. V. Minton of Elk City were in the city last Wednesday.

The proprietor of Red Front Meat Market invites you to see him. He is selling fresh meat down to bedrock . Go and try him once for good luck.

A car load of Binders and mowers were unloaded here last
Wednesday by Cross and son of Elk City. This firm is doing
extensive business in this, Elk, and Montgomery counties.
Cross and Son are the sole agent for the William Deering
And Co. Self Binders and Mowers. Also the advance Threshing
Machines. You are requested to correspond with or call on us.
Information cheerfully given.

The Chautauqua Express, City of Chautauqua Springs
W. J. Wright editor   June 1, 1888

Mayor: E. C. Purcell   Councilmen: Jake Kaufman. J. L, Stallard
J. B. Dunn, W. E. Mc Guire, A, J, Jacks, . City Clerk F. J, Fritch,
W.A. Franks Treasurer

Chautauqua County Stock Fair Association-
Pres. J. T. Pershall- Vice Pres. J. T. Smith- Sec. Lew Lynn
Treasurer- E. R. Bennett—Gen. Superintendent: Jacob Fuller

Methodist Episcopal Church: Rev. W. S. Browning pastor.
Every Sun. AM at 11:00 and 8 pm every second and fourth Sun.
Convert meetings at the parsonage every Thurs. evening.

U. B. Church   Rev. C. W. Alldredge Pastor. Services Sun. at 11am
and at 8 pm every second and fourth Sunday. Convert meeting at the
parsonage every Thurs. eve.

Union Sunday School   Meets every Sabbath morning at 10:00
Parents bring your children
W. D. Mc Guire, Supt

C.Q, G. A. R. Post 218 Meets every Sat. on or before the full moon of
each month and every two weeks thereafter. W. D. Stallard agt.   J.
W. Sipple P.C.

Chosen Friends Lodge 1.0.0.F. No. 285
Meets every Thurs. evening at their hall.
J, F. Smith N.G. , C. C. Purcell Per. Sec.,
T. J. Hawkins Rec. Sec.

Chetopa will celebrate the 4th. of July with both feet. A big
Barbecue is on the program and 6 fat beeves will meet their fate.
What are we going to do to commemorate the day?
People in great numbers are looking to Kansas this year for homes
and places in which to invest their money for well they can see that
sunny Kansas will in a few years shine more brightly than ever. Her
older sisters are watching her progress in every way with jealous
eyes.

Speaker Smith said among other things in a recent speech before the
State Board of Agriculture the atmosphere in which Kansas live is
redolent with boom, boom, boom. We hear the voice of the modest
real estate agent echo and re echo this magic word. This man that
fellow is designated as the great boomer. But he who tickles mother
earth with a hoe and causes her to laugh at harvest is the substantial
boom of the age.

William's Australian Herb Pills. If you are yellow, bilious
constipated with a headache, bad breath, drowsy, no appetite, look
out, your liver is out of order. One box of these polls will drive all
trouble away and make a new being of you. Price 25c. B, F, Barrett
agent.

Go to JT Cramer The Jeweler and have your watches, clocks, and
sewing machines repaired. Satisfaction guaranteed or no charge. All
work warranted. Office is in Post Office.

Red Front Meet Market: J. W. Harshbarger Prop.
I have just opened up a new market one door south of the Post Office
where you will always find a good supply of Choice Fresh Meats with
prices low. Everything is neat and clean. Your Patronage Solicited.

June 1, 1888

Great Bargains in Linen, Seersucker, Coats, Vests, Dusters for both
men and boys. Summer Underwear, Lawns, Vests, Summer
Underwear, Fine Dress Goods, Hose, Straw Hats, and so forth. We
are giving great bargains in these goods and it is to to your interest to

call in and see us at once. Men's and boys ready made clothing=Hats, shoes, and more are also going at bargains. Grociers and Provisions also at great bargains. Call and see us. Mc Guire Brothers.

Lawns 4.5c at Mc Guire Bros. Don't be afraid of hurting the weeds
Peace and good order reigns supreme
Don't let the weeds get the bulge on you.
Straw hats are becoming quite numerous
the air is charged with the melody of the birds.
The wheat fields present a luxucient appearance
'Whoop' for the big fourth of July celebration
Go to the lumberyard for hardware at the lowest prices
Book and machine agents are now scouring the country.
Mama buy me a pair of those fine slippers at Barretts
Screne doors at Long Bell Lumber Co Prices at the lowest
Mc Guire Bros. are in receipt of a new stock of tin ware which is marked at exceedingly loe figures. You should not fail to drop in and look through our stock if you wish anything in this line.
There will be an abundance of cherries.
Will sell you hardware lower than any firm in this city—Long Bell Lumber Co.

P 28

Sipple and Pershall dealers in Dry Goods, Clothing, Boots, Shoes, Underwear, notions,
We also carry a full line of staple and fancy groc, Provisions
   Etc. which are selling at the lowest prices. We keep in stock a full line of Drugs, Medicines, Chemicals, Oils, etc. Prescriptions carefully compounded. New fresh goods constantly arriving . you are invited to come and inspect our stock and get our prices. Sipple and Pershall CQ, Ks.

Lew Lynn-Notary Public and Justice of the Peace. Legal Papers
Drawn with neatness and dispatch. Office east side Main Street.
J. B. Beaston City Auctioneer will cry Sales in the city or country.
J. N. Goff—dealer in Harness and saddles, bridles, whips, collars, robes, brushes, combs, and in fact everything usually kept in a first class Harness Shop. Repairing neatly done.
The Express $1.00 per annum Subscribe.

CQ 6-1-1888 Local Happenings

Warm weather, no chills or fever.
Sharpen your hoe/rain or sunshine
Get ready to celebrate-new items are scarce
Strawberry short cake –corn is being cultivated
Grand prospects for fruit
Our mechanics are all busy
Let us have a great 4th
Caldwells for lawns 4c a yard
The calalpes are in full bloom
Lawns .375 cents at McGuire
Screne wire at the Lumber Yard
Dry apples and peaches at Cadwells
The cheaper the strawberry the sweeter it becomes.
Let us all celebrate at home in the best possible manner
Call at A. C. Cadwells and see his fine line of silverware
Look at those new style screne doors at Mc Guire Bros.
Best Baking Powder at Mc Guire Bro. at .15c a can, formerly .25c a can,
Call Cadwells soon and see Nain Socks, Linens, Lawns, and Prints for they are going fast.

I carry a complete line of Drugs and will not be beat in prices.
Prescriptions carefully compounded J. W. Sipple, Druggist
McGuire Bros. have just received a new lot of white dress goods, lawns, prints, muslin, and so forth which are selling for a song.
Mrs. Lee has received a new lot of millinery goods of the very latest styles. Notice the change in in her advertisement next week.
High prices has been cut square in two at Barretts. He is selling boots and shoes cheaper for cash than any other firm in Kansas"
A word to the wise is sufficient"

Remember that Sipples and Pershalls will sell you more and better goods for your money than any other firm in this country. To convince yourself you should drop in and try us.

Monroe has the nobbiest thing in the line of baking powder, a beautiful piece of glass ware is given with each piece of glassware is given with each can of the baking powder. Drop in and see them.

A car load of mowers at McGuire Bros. which are being sold on long time and slow prices, we keep repairs to all our machines and will cause you no delay in want of repair.

Screne doors for $1.25 at the Lumber Yard.

A good dress pattern at McGuire Brothrs for only 45c

Mrs. Clotfelter of Cherryvale was in the city Wednesday on business.

Paint brushes and White Wash brushes at the Lumber Yard

If you want a prescription carefully compounded go to G. L. Dunn and Co.

McGuire Bros have the most complete line of hardware in Southern Kansas.

Don't forget that Long Bell Lumber Co. will sell you hardware lower than any firm in town

Go to Sipples and Pershalls for new clean groceries. We down them all in prices, quantity.

The best washing machine in the world is now for sale at Barretts. You should step in and see them, it well worth your while .

A.C. Cadwell sells: 12# GRANULATED SUGAR FOR $1.00, #13 SNOW WHITE $1.00, #14 LIGHT BROWN $1.00.

The board of directors of the CQ co. Fair Ass. Will meet at the office of Secretary in Chautauqua Springs on Sat. 6-9 1888 at 2:00pm for the purpose of determining date of fall fair.

A full attendance is required.

Pres. J. T. Pershall   Sec. Lew Lynn

McGuire Brothers have just received a new bill of the choicest uncolored Japan tea put up in pound boxes at only 6c pd each. The tea is warranted first class Japan and the box in which it is packed is only worth 25c.

The Chautauqua Express W. J. Wright Editor. June 8, 1888

City of Chautauqua County Springs
Mayor CC Purcell
Councilmen Jake Kaufman, J. L, Stallard, J.B. Dunn.

W. E. Mc Guire, A. J. Jacks
City Clerk F. J. Fritch—Treasurer –W. A. Franks

C.Q. County Joint Stock Fair Asso.
Pres. J.T. Pershall   Vice Pres. J. T. Smith
Sec. Lew Lynn   Treas. E. R. Bennet
Gen. Superintendent Jacob Fuller

Methodist Episcopal Church-
Rev. W. S. Browning Pastor
Services every 1st and 3rd Sabbath
At 8pm. Service will begin promptly
U. E. Church
Rev. C. W. Alldredge Pastor
 Services every Sunday at 11am and at 8pm every 2nd and 4th Sunday.
Convert meeting in parsonage every Thur. evening

Union Sunday School
W. E. Mc Guire Supt.
Meeting every Sabbath at 10am Parents bring your children.

Chautauqua G. A. R. Post 218
Meets every Sat on or before the full moon of each month and every
two weeks there after. W. D. Stallard, agt, J.W. Sipple pc.

Chosen Friends Lodge 100F #285
Meets every Thurs. at their hall   J. F Smith NG—CC Purcell Per.
Secy, --- T. H. Hawkins Rec. Secy

The Plaster of Paris factories in Clark and Barber Counties are
becoming widely known for the superiority of their products. This
industry promises to develop into mammoth proportions in these
counties. Kansas to the front again.

The sugar works at Topeka are progressing steadily. The stone work
on the main building will probably be completed this week.
A large force of hands are at work. The structure will be
180x66 feet. 14 hundred acres of cane have been planted for the
factory.

A large vat is to be constructed with a capacity of 150,000 gallons of syrup.

6-8-1888

T. /j. Dunn and son –,Physicians and Surgeons , office on the west side of Main Street. Also a full line of Drugs and Chemicals. For Prescription Practice.

New Goods! Styles and price to suit the times. Hats, Ribbons, and Silk.
Tips, Flowers and laces of all descriptions. Hats, Ribbons, and Silks. A most Elegant assortment. Call and make your purchases for Fourth. Bed Rock Prices. Mrs. Mary Lee.

B. F. Barrett dealer in Boots and Shoes I have the best assortment of Boots and Shoes in Southern Kansas which I am selling at Bed Rock Prices for Spot Cash. Call and inspect my stock.

Furniture and Undertaker   T. J. Johnson, Proprietor
Col Howard will stand for the season of 1888 at the Elephant Livery Stable. P>R. Rains

Miss J. Gould rides down town in a Broadway car and goes shopping afoot. It took ten tons of paper for the new edition of Ruskins Stones of Venice. Gen. Boulanger has sold the manuscript of his book on the German invasion for $40,000.00.

Moody has given $5,000.00 and Sanky $1,000.00 toward the new Congregational Church in Northfield, Mass.

Miss Amelia Rivers is said to have been offered $30,000.00 for a new novel by NY Publishing House.

Alfred L/ Ripley, prop. Of German in Yale has resigned his position and will enter upon the banking business in Bodton.

In Western military circles Mrs. Howard is a great favorite. She dresses in a modest fashion and has unobtrusive manners. A new diamond has been discovered in Wakjra Kavor in the presidency Of Madres. It weighs over 67 carats and is valued at $75,000.00.

The N.Y. Press Club has passed a resolution for bedding the playing of any game what so ever for a money stake in the rooms of the club.

The latest fad in cigarette chromos is a picture of the Prince of Wales, John S. Sullivan, and Buffalo Bill with arms linked each smoking a cigarette.

Judge Shields of Omaha has decided that when an attorney has decided that when an attorney does not charge more money for his service than his client has, the fee is not unreasonable.

A critical Englishman who has been spending some time in NY City says that half of the citizens are honest and reputable people and the other half are politicians .

An effort is being made by the New York Working Women's Society to have the Factory inspection law amended so as to give women power to act as deputy inspectors.

Mrs. D. L. King, wife of David L. King Att. at Law in Akron, Ohio is one of the few decedents of George Washington's only sister, she being Betsy Washington's only sister, she's being Betsy Washington's great granddaughter.

Lawns 3.75c at Mc Guires Bros.

New Drugs at G. L. Dunnand co.

Screne wire at the Lumber yard

Andrew Mc Guire was at Pawhuska Mon.

S. B. Ferguson of Kansas City registered at the CQ House Mon.

Alfred Canville was in the city Wed last week.

Will Scott of Indy was in town Tues.

Dr. Kennedy of the Agency was in the city last Frid.

W. F. Rodimal of Sedan was in town one day last week.

Dr. Dalby of Jonesburg was in city Sat. on ---

A.C. Cadwell has his store room windows handsomely painted.

Andrew McGuire went down to the Osage Agency Sat on business

J. T. Pershall and George Edwards went down to Pawhuska last week on business.

Charles Fagan of the agency registry at the CQ House last Mon.

S. E. Booth who has been in the city for a week past went to Moline a few days ago.

R. K. Black and Att. Price of Peru were pleasant callers at the office last Wed.

W. A. Franks, lumberman went down to the Osage Agency last Tues. eve. Elder J. C. Ross and Joe Futhey of Havana were in the city Sun in Att at the Childrens Day Picnic. Joe in company with Rev. Allridge was a pleasant caller at this office.

Albert Campbell of Havana was visiting CQ last Tues and wed.

Rev. Browning had the misfortune of severely cut his foot last week by acc stepping on an open pocket knife.

S H Pershall who resides about 3 miles E of town lost a valuable colt one day last week it having fallen into an empty well.

I E Imel late of Coyville has moved into the Fuller property at the South end of Main St. where he has a livery stock

Ike is a rustler and we hope will meet with good success

R. K. Black has retired from the editorial charge of the Peru Call having leased the same to Mr. Gynn of that place

6-15-1888   CQ Express

City of Chautauqua Springs
Mayor: C. C. Purcell.
Councilmen: Jake Kaufman, J. L. Stallard, J. B. Dunn,
W. E. Mc Guire, and A. J. Jacks
City Clerk: F. T. Fritch,
Treasurer: W. A. Franks

Chautauqua County Joint Stock Fair Association:
President: J.T. Pershall
Vice President: J. T. Smith
Secretary: Lew Lynn
Treasurer: E. R. Bennet
General Superintendent: Jacob Fuller

Methodist Episcopal Church
Pastor: Reverend C. W. Alldredge

G. A. R. Chautauqua Post #218
Meets every Sabbath at 10:00am or Saturday on or before
the full moon of each month and every two weeks thereafter.
W.D. Stallard ag.   J.W. Sipple P.C.

Union Sunday School meets every Sabbath A. M. at 10:00
Parents bring your children

U.R. Church   Reverend C. W. Alldredge, Pastor

Services every Sunday morning 11:00 a.m. and 9 p.m. every second and fourth Sunday. Convert meeting at the parsonage Thursday evening.

Methodist Episcopal Church Reverend W. S. Browning pastor.
Services every first and third Sabbath at 3:00 pm
Services will begin promptly.

Chosen Friend Lodge 100F   No. 285
Meets every Thursday evening at their hall.
j. F. Smith -NG   C. C. Purcell- personal secretary
T.H. Hawkins- Personal Secretary—T.H. Hawkins-Recording Sec.

Times may be dull and money scarce but with all that know eastern man need to be afraid to immigrate to Kansas if he has the   means to land him here and enough to keep himself and family for the first few months. Homes can be bought or rented cheap and farmers, merchants, and tradesmen and professional   men have an open field before them here.
I have taken a great verity   of views which will be an exhibition when I return to the Springs. T.M. Concannon.
Prospects for crops and fruit continue to be promising and Pawhuska is a small Garden of Eden.
In the last few days the different towns along the State Line have been represented – Ark City, Elgin, Cedar Vale, Sedan,, Chautauqua, and Caney have been represented; some on business, some on fishing, hunting, and some for rest and some for pleasure trips with their families.

We had a little excellent day this week. The Marshall succeeded in capturing some men and their outfits. They had with them a large amount of what Indians call 'fire water'. They are   prisoners here now at the Agency and from the instructions I heard the agent giving the marshals, I think it will be sometime before they engage in the business again.

Another vehicle loaded with camping equipment rushed through town yesterday and as the agent thought it looked suspicious an officer was sent after them and brought them back and the wagon was searched but it was a 'water haul'.

J. Dunn and Son   Physicians ans Surgeons.
Office on Main Street. Also full line of Drugs and Chemicals for prescription practice.

New Good Styles and Prices to suit the times. Hats, Ribbons, Silks, Tips, Flowers, Laces of all descriptions. A most elegant display. Call and make your purchases for Forth!
Bed Rock Prices! Mrs. Mary Lee.

B.F. Barrett Boots and Shoes. I have the best assortment of Boots and Shoes Kansas which I am selling at Bed Rock Prices for Spot Cash. Call and inspect my stock.

Furniture and Undertaker   T. J. Johnson, proprietor
I have just received a large and well selected stock of furniture, chairs, sofas, bed steads, stands, tables, mattress and so forth which I will sell at the lowest cash price. Call and see me.

Colonel Howard will stand for season of 1888 at the Elephant Livery Stable. P.R. Rains

Patti says she has more wealth than she will need but of fame she will never have enough.

Ruskin has written 64 books and his annual receipts from his publisher reach $20,000.00.

Mrs. Garrett Anderson, the leading   woman physician of England makes $50,000.00 a year.

Smith College will get more than $100,000.00 under the will of George W. Hubbard.

Alexander 3 Emperor of all Russia is around borrowing again. This time he wants 500,000,000 rubles.

Prince Oscar of Sweden and his bride Carlsorons, their future residence in the south of Sweden. They are now known as the Prince and Princess Bernadotta.

Joseph Davis of Wayne County West Virginia has a daughter aged six years who weighs 230 pounds. This is believed to be the largest child of it's age in the world.

George B. Roberts President of the Penn. Rail Road system has been in the companies service since 1851. His first employment being a Rodman in the engineer corps.

A new material called 'Leatherine' is an English manufacture. It can be sold at 5c or 6c pound and is said to be as tough as leather and is designed for packing and bagging.

The statement is made that no less than 6 species of North American birds have become extinct during the last ten years and it is claimed that the English Sparrow were the main cause.

The Engineer says there is no properly recorded instance of a locomotive ever attaining the speed of eighty miles per hour and quotes Charles R. Martin as saying that higher speeds are mythical.

June 22, 1888

City of Chautauqua Springs, Kansas :
Mayor: C. C. Purcell
Councilmen: Jake Kaufman, J. L. Stallard, J. B. Dunn,
W. E. Mc Guire, A. J. Jacks. F. J. Fritch: City Clerk,
W. A. Franks, Treasurer

C.Q. County Joint Stock Association.
President: J. T. Pershall, Vice President: J. I. Smith
Sec. Lew Lynn, Treasurer: E. R. Bennet
General Supervisor: Jacob Fuller

Methodist Episcopal Church
Reverend W. S. Browning, Pastor

Services every first and third Sabbath at 8 p.m. Services will begin promptly. Everyone invited.

U. B. Church
Reverand C. W. Alldredge, Pastor
Services every Sunday at 11 a.m. and at 8 p.m. every second and 4th. Sunday. Convert meeting at parsonage every Thursday evening.

Union Sunday School meets every Sabbath a.m. at 10:00. Parents bring your children.   W.E. McGuire, Supt.

Chautauqua G.A.R. Post No. 218
Meets every Saturday on or before the full moon of each month and every two weeks there after. W.D. Stallard- AGT., J.W. Sipple P.C.

Chosen Friends Lodge 100F   No. 285 Meets every Thursday evening at their hall. J. F. Smith N.G.,   C. C. Purcell Per. Secy
T.H. Hawkins Rec. Secy.

R. R. Time Table
Chicago, Kansas, and Western Rail Road
Pass. Going E.   at 8:35
Pass. Going W.   at7:15
Freight going E. at 1:05
Freight going W. at 7:45
Passenger trains run daily, Sunday included.
Freight trains run daily except Sundays

Go to J. T. Cramer the Jeweler
And have your watches, clocks, and sewing machines repaired.
Satisfaction guaranteed or no charge. All work warranted.
Office in Post Office.

Newspaper learned of the elopement of Doctor W. Woodring and Mrs. Nichodemus both of Elk City. Dr. Woodring is one of the first settlers of Montgomery County and for a number of years practiced to practice medicine in Louisburg township where he is highly respected. Mrs. N. is a handsome young widow with considerable means and was also highly respected by all who knew her.

Her husband died three or four years ago and Doctor was appointed Administer of his estate and in attending to the affairs of the estate he was thrown considerably in Mrs. N's. company which has proven to be an elopement. The family of Dr. consisted of a wife and two boys who were visiting relatives and it was generally supposed that the doctor was attending medical school in Saint Louis. Mrs. N. was disposed of and she went to Kansas City but stated that she was going East to visit friends where Dr. Woodring joined her and they knowing that they should be discovered if the remained there and he returned to Elk City and deeded his property to his wife stating that he had gone a friends' security and he was about to fail, then he told her that he had accepted a position as ail Road Surgeon in a town in Kansas City and in the company of his frail female friend who was about to become a mother and started to Texas. His relatives did not hear from him and grew uneasy about him and wrote to the town which he was to locate himself but nothing was learned of him, but from what said it is evident that he is in Old Mexico out of reach of the law and justice. Elk City is all distracted over the affair.

J. T. Dunn and son, Physician and Surgeon
Office on west side of Main Street. Also a full line of Drugs and Chemicals for Prescription Practice.

New Goods! New Goods! Styles and prices to suit the times. Hats—Ribbons—Silks—Tips—Flowers—Laces of all descriptions, a most Elegant Assortment. Call and make your purchase for the Forth! Bed Rock Prices. Mrs. Mary Lee.

Boots and Shoes   B. F. Barrett
I have the best assortment of Boots and Shoes in Southern Kansas which I am selling at Bed Rock Prices for Spot Cash. Call and inspect my stock.

Furniture and Undertaker   T. J. Johnson, Proprietor
I have just received a large and well selected stock of furniture consisting of Chairs, Safes, Sofas, Bed, Spreads, Stands, Tables, Mattresses,, etc. Which I will sell at the lowest Cashes price. Call me and see me.

Col. Howard standing at the Elephant Livery Stable. P. R. Rains. Mae Wilson, daughter of M. Grevy, x President to France is to remove to New York to live.

Lt. John W. Graydon, the inventor of the dynamite shell projectile is dangerously ill with a brain infection in Washington.

P A O-Y U N, President of Pekin Academy is translating Shakespeare for the benefit of youthful princes of the Chinese Imperial House.

James Red path is now in Richmont Va. Recovering from his recent langerosis illness, but he will probably not resume literary work for several months.

A charming figure at the recent private view of the Grosvernor Gallary was Miss Kate Greenway in a green plush gown, a figured silk shawl and a green trimmed hat.

Mrs. Ruth McEnery Stuart, the latest writer of Negro dialect stories lives in New Orleans. She is a young woman, tall, dark haired, and fine looking. She has only recently taken up literary work.

Seven year old Willie McConnell of San Francisco found a bottle of whisky and tasted it's contents. He liked it and drank over half a pint. He became tipsy then ill and in a few hours died in great agony in spite of the best efforts of the good doctor to save him.

Thomas Eggleston has just died at Speerlockville, West Virginia at the advanced age of one hundred twelve years. There was never a day since he was 16 years old that he was without his pipe and he said he fully believed his life was prolonged by use of tobacco.

The Turkish Governor has a suspicion that Russian pilgrims who just now are arriving in great numbers at the monasteries at the Galatea and Mount Athoe are really come to spy out the country and have given orders that the pilgrims be closely watched and hustled along as rapidly as possible.

It is said that canaries and other birds may be freed from insects by placing a white cloth over the cage at dusk. During the night the insects will leave the birds for the cloth and in the morning they can be destroyed by placing the cloth in hot water. A repetition of the process will soon clear away the pests.

At Black River Falls, Wins, a 14 year old girl and a 16 year old boy was married with the consent of the parents. At the hour fixed for the wedding the bridegroom was playing ball and as soon as the ceremony was over he went back to his game while the bride resumed her interrupted play with some of the neighboring girls.

A Chicagoan owns a Siberian Blood Hound of 183 pounds.

The Romeo Hydrant is the title of a Michigan paper.

Tallulah Ga. Is so healthy that the nearest doctor lives 12 miles away.

A parrot that was valued at $3,000.00 died in Poughkeepale? recently. It could sing, talk, and swear in the English, Dutch, and Portuguese Languages.

John Jacob Astor has presented the Astor Library a lot of land in Lafayette place adjoining that institution so that may control the nearest neighbors and be better protected in case of fire.

A young Russian nobleman was in a tailors shop in Paris trying on a garment when a pistol fell out of his pocket and went off. The bullet wounded him mortally in the lower part of his stomach and he died a few hours later.

A fat woman is a chairful creature. Washing Post

A young lady has named one of her admirers-HoosacTunnel because he is such an everlasting bore. Warren Mirror.

Purcell and Beaston Real Estate and Exchange Agents
Farms, Raw Lands, Stock Ranches for sale and trade.

Merchandise to exchange for lands.

Lunch and Ice Cream Parlor
George Vaughn prop. I also carry a full line of candies, nuts, Canned Goods—Third door South of Post Office. Chautauqua, Kansas

J. N. Goff.   Harness, Saddles, Bridles, Whips, Collars, Robes, Combs, and in fact everything kept in a first class Harness Shopp. Repairing Neatly Done.

C. C. Purcell's Brokers Office
Office on main street Chautauqua, Kansas

Community Hotel   J. E. Baker prop.
First Class $1.00 per day. Good clean beds and rooms and tables furnished with the best market affords.

Clotfelter and Booth prop of The Elephant Livery Stable Good rigs, good saddles horses furnished at the most reasonable prices. We run a Daily Hack to and from the Osage Agency, Indian Territory . S share of your patronage solicited.

The Chautauqua Express June 29, 1888   W. J. Wright

We observe that traveling Frauds and Confidence men are victimizing several persons in adjoining counties. Their manner of operation is as varied as the customers. A good thing to do is this: buy nothing of strangers that you can get at hoome and under no circumstances sign a paper of any kind offered you. by a person whom you do not know. A strict observance of these rules would send the fraud to jail or to work while the good people would not have to pay so many debts that they never contracted . Buy your goods at home.

Radway's Pills- The great Liver and Stomach Remedy-Paines Celery Compound. The Nervous, The Aged, and the Depilated.

An American hog however well dressed is not allowed the freedom of German society. It's different in this country. Pasadena Union

Chautauqua Express   W. J. Wright   6-29-1888

B.S. Mc Guire has made application for the principal ship of the public schools in Chautauqua Springs.

Sioole and Pershall-Dry goods- groceries
Drugs, Medicines, Chemicals,

Lew Lynn   Justice of the Peace
Office East side Main Street

J. B. Beaston—City or Country   Auctioneers
Cigars, Tobacco, and Notions

Local Happenings
Peaches are fine—Wheat about to be cut—Hurrah for the 4th.!—Weather somewhat warm—Warm days but cool nights—Hurrah for the glorious 4th—Some fine apples in the market—The 4th. of July is close upon us—This is exceedingly fine growing weather—The hum of the threshing machine is next in order—Work on the new church is now progressing nicely—We printed some fine cards, for George Vaughn this week—The streets of our thriving little city were crowded last Sat.—Several of our exchanges are now boasting of having roasting ears—W. E. Rodimel of Sedan was in the city Sat. attending the big stock salle—T.D. Mc Brain of Sedan will address the many people here on the 4th of July.—Ed Linebough of Sedan was in the city Sat. and made this office a call.—John Romick, the genial prop. Of the Chautauqua House left orders for 1000 note heads at this office Mon.—Thomas Concannon writes us that he will return to Chautauqua before the 4th and will be ready to photograph everything and anything.

A drunken Chinaman was seen on Broadway New York the other day. If they are going to become civilized as that it is time that they were kept out of the country.   Leavenworth Times

J. A. Brown of Caney was in the city Sat.

James Koonce of Sedan was in our town Sat.

J, E. Baker -   Groceries and Flour

W.G. Glynn of Topeka was in the city Monday.

B.V. Morton of Elk City was in the city Tues.

Will Wylie of Wichita, Kan. was in the city Frid.

E. M. Matthews of Pawhuska was in the city Sun.

M. R. Cowden of Coffeyville was in the city Tues.

Edna Williams of Independence was in the city Frid.

E. S. Strong of Wichita was in town last Frid.

G. W. Schlegel of Fredonia was in town Mon.

S. H. Hamilton of Elk City was in the city Mon.

Charles Tinker of Osage Agency was in the city Sat.

Jas. P. Trimmer of Bloomington, Ill. was in town Frid.

George H. Williams and family was in the city Sat.

Robert Gillstrap, William Cooper, and C. N. Prudom of the Agency were in town Sun.

Peru is going to celebrate the 4th. in shape of a picnic basket picnic Some of their bills are in town giving the full program.

The Mayor has issued a proclamation calling a special bond election to be held on July 9th. to vote $1,500.00 improvement bonds.

The big stock sale which was advertised for last Sat. was attended by people from all over the county and a goodly number from the nation.

J. T. Cramer, the Jeweler, has removed his tools into the building two doors down south of the Post Office where he will continue to repair watches, clocks, and so forth.

The Havana Herald is copying from us will here after please quote us correctly. In the article copied from us last week the Harold has at least a half dozen words set that were not in the original articles "Missouri" quote was correctly "Chautauqua will celebrate at the city park and fair grounds a grand Barbecue in which all will be provided for. Good speakers, and good music will be in attendance. Exciting Indian Race will take place at the Fair Grounds at 2:00 pm. A Grand Indian War Dance will be the promised feature. Everyone is invited! COME !

Chautauqua Express   W.J. Wright- Editor July 6, 1888

George Vaughn went to Independence Monday.

Miss Dorpha Slater went over to Havana Tuesday.
Ed Hopper of Hewins went over to Sedan last Tues. on business.

Lew Lynn went over to Sedan last Tues. on business.

Andrew McGuire went to Independence Tues.

Reverend Browning made a trip over to Cherryvale yesterday.

A. L, Arlington of New York City were in the city yesterday.

C. A. Meigs and lady of Longton were in town yesterday.

Rev. Browning sports a new cane, a present from his sister in law.

Dr. Hawkins returned home from Kansas City Thursday evening.

Tom Concannon came up from the Agency last Monday evening.

J. D. McBrian of Sedan registered at the Chautauqua House Wednesday.

Rev. Alldredge sold J. T. Ross of Havana two lots in the city of Chautauqua.

William Bowles and lady of Elgin registered at the Chautauqua House Wed.

People from all over the country were here on the 4th. and everyone enjoyed themselves hugely.

J. G. Kaufman of Chicago was in the city on business this week and returned home this morning.

G. W. Schlegel of Fredonia is in the city partaking of the wonderful Mineral Waters for his health.

If you want hardware at the lowest price you can save money by purchasing at Long Bell Lumber Company.

Just received at McGuire Brothers new invoice of screne doors and wire. These goods are selling cheaper than any firm in southern Kansas. Call and see us.

Screne doors at the Lumber Yard at the lowest figures.

Our little city was thrown in a great stage of excitement last Monday night over the sudden disappearance of a promenade lady. Mr.— On returning home from his daily labors found his wife absent but supposed that she had just stepped over to the neighbors. Waiting until a late hour and she still was not home he went around the neighbor hood searching for her he was told she had quickly stated she was going to the dry goods store Sipple and Pershalls buying her 4th. of July dress goods, ribbons, fans, Parasol, and so forth before they were all gone.

Rev. Gray will commence a series of meetings at this place on Friday evening July 13 and will continue aver Sunday. Everybody cordially invited to attend.

The knobbiest thing in the fruit jar line is now for sale. McGuire Brothers.

The Havana Herold was one year old last Friday. E. J. Barron, the editor and prop. Has sold the entire office, subscription books, and so forth to E. G. Smith of that place. Mr. Smith is an energetic young man and by his close attention to business we perdict that he will make a success of the undertaking.

Real Estate Transfers reported by C. C. Purcell.

Lot 6 block 8 from W. A. Franks to G. W. Jones.

Lot 5 block 1 Kiles Add from G. W. Jones to W. A. Franks.

Lot 6 block 8 from W. A. Franks to G. W. Jones.

Lots 1, 3, 5, 7, block 10 and lots 10 and 12 block 19 from Stephan Johnson and G. W. Woolsey to R. W. Payne.

Se ¼ Sec. 22 Tp 34, R12, from Purcell and Beaston and Nicolls to Dillon.

146/1?2 of the Ne ¼ of the Ne ¼ Sec 13, Tp 35, R11 from Purcell and Beaston and Nicolls and Dillon.

Joseph Jefferson according to his wife and son went last week to his country home on Buzzar's Bay, Mass.

Boxing and slugging are looked to become a dead letter in Pittsburg. At least the authorities there express their intention of dealing out such fate.

Marshall Livingstone Perria of Harvard 1874 and of Gottingen has been appointed instructor in the European languages at Boston University.

Reverend Dr. William C. Winslow of Boston and the Egyptian exploration fund will deliver the annual address at St. Johns' College in Annapolis, Md. On June 27.

The weighing machine in hotels and other public places in Philadelphia are said to average a net profit of $25.00 per month.

Empress Elizabeth of Austria has been forbidden to take equine exercise for some months now amuses herself with a tricycle.

The Mormon hierarchy is said to pay A. M. Gibson a salary of $10,000.00 a year to look after the interests of Zion at Washington.

When Charter Dickens Jr. reached Portland, Oregon last Tuesday he had made a 27,ooo mile lecture tour through the United States.

General Wade Hampton was thrown from his horse in Washington the other day and suffered a compound fracture of his wooden leg.

Soft Maple Trees planted on dry land and cultivated produce as much sap as rock maple and delicious sugar can be made from it.

Oliver Wendell Holmes Jr., Justice of the Supreme Court of Mass. Is visiting in California and will closely study the Chinese cheap labor question.

It is said $15,000,000.00 worth of tile has been laid in Illinois and that if the tile is placed in a continuess line it would reach around the globe.

Alonzo Steele of Grinnell, Iowa has given $20,000.00 to endow the chair of Mathematics and National Philosophy of Iowa College, the Chair to be called in memory of his daughter the Myra Steele' Chair.

Boots and Shoes – B. F. Barrett, I have the best assortment of boots and shoes in Southern Kansas which I am selling at Bed Rock Prices for Spot Cash. Call and inspect my stock.

Furniture and Undertaker supplies. T. J. Johnson.

The Elephant Livery Stable- Coltfelter and Booth and Goodring Good Saddle Horses furnished at the most reasonable prices. We run Daily Hack to and from the Osage Agency in Indian Territory. A share of your Patronage Solicited.

T. J. Dunn and Son- Physicians and Surgeons. Office on West side of Main Street. We also sell a full line of drugs and chemicals for prescriptions.

C. C. Purcell-- Notary Public
John B. Beaston: Farms, Ranch Lands and Stock Ranches For Sale or Trade. Merchandise to exchange for lands.

Lunch and Ice Cream Parlor- George Vaughn Prop. A full line of Candies, Nuts, Canned Goods, Cigars, Tobaccos, and Pop.
Third door South of Post Office, Chautauqua, Kansas

Big Bargains in Clothing, Groceries, and Provisions.

Chautauqua Mineral Springs/ Bath House
Stephen Johnson Proprietor
Hot or Cold Baths 25c   Electric Baths 50c
Chautauqua Springs, Kansas

July 13, 1888

Local Happenings:

J. T. Pershall is on the sick list.

V. Harris of Elgin was in town Friday

G. W. Schlegel went to Fredonia Wed.

S. B. Foster of Sedan was in the city Sat.

C. Carpenter of Elgin was in our city last Frid.

E. A. Benson of Topeka was in the city Sat.

W. W. Barr of Chicago was in the city Sat.

C. Steipel of Kansas City was in the city Friday Last.

Mrs. Mary Lee was illthe first part of the week.

George Edwards made a trip to Havana last Tuesday.

Theo Kincaid of Marshall, Mo. was in the city Sunday.

Daiel Wassam of Independence was in the city Tues.

A. C. Cadwell is suffering from an attack of Rheumatism.

L. A. Millapaugh of Saint Joe, Mo. was in the city Wed.

M. Rogers and lady of Jonesburg were in the city last Frid.

George N. Williams of Terre Haute was in town last Frid.
James Monroe went down to Independence the first of the week.

Joe Gravely, the rustling traveling agent for the Santa Fe was in the city last Sat.

W. A. Franks is the unfortunate possessor of a felon on the thumb of his right hand.

John Quinn of Caney was in the city Tues. and made the office a pleasant call.

W. E. McGuire in company with D.E. Wassam went down to Pawhuska last Tues.

David Ellis, the popular grocery man of Peru came down on the train last Tues. eve.

Mrs. Rosa Love and two little children of Bronson, Kansas have been visiting for a week past.

J. W. Darnall of Jonesburg was among the many who registered at the Chautauqua House Sat. last.

George Vaughn has had a new counter placed in his lunch room. He also sports a new Indian Cigar sign.

Ed Oliver who has been in the city on business for a month past. He left his home in Fayetteville Ark. last month.

Joe Futhey of Havana was in the city Sunday. Joe makes quite frequent visits to our city as the center of attraction for many of the young men.

Add Locals:

Boom, fire flies, keep cool, new wheat, midsummer, hot weather, money tight, farmers busy, don't over heat, weeds growing, shortening days, apple dumplings, politicians active, oats are ripening, stockmen nervous, produce market active, early apples are plenty, 1888 is about half spent, corn reaching skyward, exterminate the weeds, the hay crop is abundant, the milkshake is popular, daylight begins to shorten, Sat. was lively as usual, potatoes promise a good crop, do not hitch horses to shade tree, most of the corn is tasseled out, the Bath House is a good institution.

Farm machinery is in demand this year,
The Threshing Machines are harvesting.
The political pot will soon begin to boil.
Watermelons will soon be in the market.
Don't worry, don't fret, and you'll stay cool.

Walnut logs continue a staple commodity.

The festive flies have become more numerous.

Black berries and wild plums are plenty this season.

The great white clouds of summer are now rolling by.

The next three months are the hot months of the year.

No part of the man will stand so many blows as his nose.

We are in the 112 years of Independence and American Freedom.

Watermelon will soon be putting in it's appearance at the markets.

Mrs. Betsy Aversill of Conn. who has just celebrated her 101 birthday and reads without glasses.

Mrs. Sarah Rothchild of Chicago celebrated her one hundredth birthday by dancing a minuet the other day.

Charles H. Hackly, a millionaire lumber man of Muskegon, Michigan has given $100,000.00 to the Public Library of that city.

Inspector Byrnes of New York Police becomes Chief Inspector and the salary of his office has been raised to $5,000.00.

Mrs. Fair of California prefers her own palace car and cook to the best hotel between New York and San Francisco.

Mrs. John Sherwood repudiates the etiquette which demands that a lady should bow to a gentleman before he can presume to bow.

The wife of Senator Palmer has set the fashion at Washington of holding Sunday evening, parties which are entertained by sacred music.

A French writer classes all women by the size of their thumbs. Those with large thumbs are said to be more likely to possess native intelligence while the small thumbs indicate feeling.

July 20, 1888

City of Chautauqua Mayor C. C. Russell
Councilmen: Jake Kaufman, J. L. Stallard, J. B. Dunn, W. E. McGuire   Treasurer: W. A. Franks

Chautauqua County Joint Stock Fair Ass.
Pres. J. T. Pershall
Vice President J. T. Smith
Sec. Lew Lynn
Treasure E. R. Bennett
Gen. Superintendent   Jacob Fuller

Chetopa has passed an ordinance prohibiting boys under fifteen years of asge from appearing on the streets after 8pm. If this regulation prevailed in every town in Kansas it would not be necessary to build an additional penitentiary in that state for some years. Kansas City Star.

Additional Local

Sat hot, Flax ripening, some sickness, new buildings, ripe tomatoes, new time tables, hot? travel increasing, everything lovely, corn doing nicely, some few chiggers, we sell old papers, merchant smiling, black berries scares, potatoes, are 35c, roasting ears on deck, where is our jeweler? Spring chickens are nice, oats are being harvested, streets crowded Sat., apples are worth but 40c patronize home institution, the threshing machine is kept busy, wheat is running a large yield this year, the Edna Star has suspended publication, can you get up early enough to get on the early train?, they tell us that our 'watch tinker' has pulled his freight, The Edna Star has suspended publication, the swing business is booming for J. Kaufman, Remember the big Excursion on the third of August, the rustle of the growing corn is sweet music,

Union SS Excursion to Chautauqua Springs is Aug. 3rd.No postponement. Get ready Independence Tribune.
The first new wheat shipped into Kansas City this year. It was clean, large, and solid and found a ready market at good figures.

Just think of upland in Finny County turning out 75 bushels of oats to the acre. What is the state of Kansas coming to anyway?
Havana Harold.

Chautauqua House   J. C. Romick prop.
This house has been refurnished throughout. Everything neat and clean. Traveling guests will find pleasant entertainment. Coolest and most pleasant rooms in Southern Kansas.

The United States Man of War was sold in Brooklyn navy yard a few days ago $10.00.

The largest flour mill in the world will be established in Duluth. The capacity will be 6,000 barrels per day.

It costs South Carolina $75,000.00 a year to pension those disabled and the widows of those killed in the late war.

Walter R. Warren of Brooklyn is suffering with some disease closely resembling hydrophobia caused by the bite of a man.

Roan Dog, the big medicine man of the Sioux finding his mother dead and his reputation gone sent a bullet through his heart last week.

The four leading female colleges in the U. S. are Wellesley with 620 students, Vassar with 283 students, Smith 367, and Bryn-Mawr with 71.

A Patriotic old New Yorker says that if it wasn't for it's dog days and cat nights New York in summer would be an ideal place of residence.

It is announced that after settling all outstanding debts theee estate of the late Roscoe Conkling will amount to between $700,000.00 and $800.000.00.

Railways are said to consume more than half of world's products of iron, the car wheels required in the U. S. alone taking more than 2,000,000 tons.

Matthew W. Sadam, an eccentric old man who died at Terre Haute Indiana last week was buried in a coffin which foe 25 years he had kept in his bedroom.

Daniel Wesson of Independence was in town Thursday.

Andrew McGuire was at Kansas City the first of week.

J. T. Pershall is reported to be recovering from a sick spell.

Judge Petit of the Agency was in town first of week.

Will Scott of Independence was in city Tues.

The Longton Times came out last week with a full page ad.

Wheat about all stacked.

Corn marching right along.

The hay crop will be large.

We went to Havana Sat.

Another sprinkle Sat. night.

Mrs. Sipple was in Caney Tues. last.

The mercury is rising near the top.

Who won the cigars in the foot race?

The new livery barn is now running orders.

Candidates will soon begin making their canvess.

We printed some letter heads for Lew Lynn this week.

Daniel Wassan of Independence was in town Tues.

Mrs. Lee who has been seriously ill is rapidly improving.

J. T. Pershall is reported as recovering from his sick spell.

Andrew McGuire was in Kansas City the first part of the week.

Judge Petit of the Agency was in town the first of the week.

Will Scott of Independence was in the city again last week.

The Longton Times came out last week with a full page advertisement.

W. F. Rodimel of Sedan was a pleasant caller at this office Tues. last.

Nearly all the wheat has been stacked and without any damage resulting from the rains.

The Cedar Vale Star last week contained a full page advertisement. The Star is getting there.

A sickly season is upon us. Buy your drugs from Sipple and Pershall and always get the pure and fresh.

Now what is starting out in the market at 60cis too low. The farmers who can do so should hold their wheat.

Mr. Menroe has sold his team and buggy to I. F. Imel who has now a good livery outfit and will be found at Monroe's old stand.

Ben Foster and John Frazier of Havana came over last Tues. evening and are now working at the big yard near the depot.

Miles Love of Bronson, Kansas came over last week and accompanied his wife who has been visiting with us to Havana where they will visit a few days and then return to their home in Bourbon County.

J. R. Lawson of Elgin was in the city last Saturday.

John Lee of Sedan was in the city Tuesday.

Albert Campbell of Havana is visiting us this week.

J. E. Baint of Pawhuska was in the city last Monday.

G. W. Schlegel returned from Fredonia last Tuesday.

E. B. Strickland of Saint Joe was in the city last Monday.

A. C. Cadwell is still confined to his room with rheumatism.

E. C. Pennell of Senee, Kansas was in the city Tuesday.

Charles Fagan of the Osage Agency was in town last Saturday.

C. C. Percell registered at the Chautauqua House last Tuesday.

A number of parties from Elk City are visiting I. E. Imel and family.

George H. Williams of Independence was in the city Monday last.

W. N. Anderson of the C. K. and W. Railroad was in the city Saturday last.

Wanted: to rent a two bedroom dwelling house. If you have a house to rent of this kind call at this office.

Those who desire to join the base ball club are requested to meet at the lumber yard at 2 o'clock.

Mrs. Williams and family who have been visiting relatives in the city for some time just returned to Independence Wednesday.
Died- Park, infant son of Rev. and Mrs. Alldredge at their residence in the city last Wednesday morning.

The first kerosene lamp is treasured by a Maine woman. But the first kerosene can left the country with the servant girl who discovered how to build a quick fire.

Jack Raufman says he has a nice window in the south side of the post office. We took notice of the hole in the south side of the building but just supposed the rats had cut it to get out.

J. E. Baker has torn down the wire fence on the South side of his hotel and replaced it with pickets. He completed the hotel by cutting a window a little larger than Kaufman's in the South side of the hotel.

If even Kansas promises more and better corn than at presant it is so far back that we are unable to recollect it. It would have to be very dry and hot accompanied by grass hopper invasion to prevent a good corn crop.

Dr. Kennedy went to Sedan Wensday in responce to a telegram from a man in Texas stating that he would be at Sedan on or about the 17th. with Ed Morgan for who the doctor is offering a reward of $300.00.

The new rail road time table does not seem to meet with the approval of all our citizens. The way the train now runs it makes it very inconvenient for the post master, mail carrier, bus man, and so forth. We hope it will not remain this way long.

The following delegates were elected to attend the Republican County Convention at Sedan Saturday July 21, 1888

Delegates:	Alternates
Lew Lynn	R. C. Johnson
S. T. Hartzell	William Burriss
W. A. Price	T. B. Darnell
S. S. Edmunson	John Gurley
W. Stallard	J. T. Smith

Sheriff's Sale

On the 31st. day of July 1888 at 2 o'clock pm at Chautauqua Springs in Bellville township in Chautauqua County, State of Kansas I will sell at a Public Auction the following property to wit. One light bay mare, 4 years old, One open roan mare 4 years old, one open top buggy, one set of light double harness, the property of J. J. Holden, taken on order of attachment in favor of William Prilliman

J. J. Adams, Sheriff
R. C. Johnson Deputy Sheriff
First publication   July 20, 1888

Publication Notice

A. C. Cadwell   Before Lew Lynn- Justice of the Peace.
                                 Belleville township, Chautauqua, County

    Vs

The said dependents are hereby notified that on the 6th. day of July 1888 an order of attachment for the sum of thirty nine dollars and sixty cents was issued by the above named Justice of the Peace against their goods in the above entitled action and that said cause will be heard on the 18th. day of August at 10 o'clock am.

A. C. Cadwell: plaintiff
Attest: Lew Lynn Justice of the Peace.

JULY 27, 1888

CITY OF CHAUTAUQUA BOARD

Mayor: C. C. Purcell

Councilmen Jake Kaufman, J. L. Stallard, J. B. Dunn,
W. E. McGuire, A. Jack, City Clerk: F. J. Fritch
Treasure: W. A. Franks

Chautauqua State Fair Association:

M.E. Church:

U. B. Church:

Union 53

Chautauqua G. A. R.

Chosen Friends Lodge:

Rail Road Time Table:

Chicago, Kansas, and Western Rail Road

Eastern bound -
Passenger leaves at 7:31 am
Freight leaves at 1:25 pm

West bound
Passenger leaves at 7:09 pm
Freight leaves at 8:09 pm

Passenger train runs daily except Sunday

July 27, 1888

Additional Local:

Base ball, Good Apples, Water Melons, Nice tomatoes, July almost gone, Moon light nights, Strangers numerous, More rain, more corn, Sweet potatoes growing, Wasn't it hot Saturday?, Water melon season has arrived, The ripest fruit will not fall into your mouth, Fruit of all kinds will be abundant, The Kansas farmer will this year make a big jump toward getting out of debt, Cherryvale is suffering from the worst disease yet known, Salvation Army, Kansas farmers will have no trouble this year to pay off mortgages and make additional improvements.

It is rumored that large amounts of counterfeit gold and silver coins are in circulation in Kansas.

A New York cigar manufacturing put out a sign ' Good strippers wanted' and was overran with variety actresses seeking engagements.

The prospect of a cotton crop in the county is said to be more flattering than of the past years, and unless soon unforeseen mishap befalls it the crop will simply be immense. Sedan Graphic.

If anybody knows anything that would be of any use to any body or any news item from the country come right into our office and spit it out. We will round them off and pass them to our residents.

The Chautauqua Springs Express under the editorial management of Mr. Wright is one of the spiciest little local papers that comes to this print shop and from all indications we wound judge that thr Express is receiving a liberal patronage. It certainly deserves it. Sedan Grapic.

Chautauqua House   J. C. Romick Proprietor
Good Sample Rooms

T. J, Dunn and Son: Physicians and Surgeons
Office on West side of Main Street.
Furniture and Undertaker T. J. Johnson

The Elephant Livery Stable

Clotfelter and Booth. Osage Agency Indian Territory

J. N. Goff—Harness and Saddles

Monroe and Company—Groceries, Flour, Cigars, and Tobacco.

C. C. Purcell's- Brokers Office off Main street Chautauqua, Kansas

B. F. Barrett—Boots and Shoes

Sipple and Pershall—Dry Goods.

Lew Lynn – Notary Public and Justice of the Peace.
Office East side of Main Street

J. B. Beaston—City Councilman.
Office: Main Street, Chautauqua Springs, Kansas

J. E. Baker-Groceries, Flour, and Provisions

Local Happenings:
James Purcell of Nevada is in the city. J. B. Lawson of Elgin was in the city Sunday, John J. Hardin of St. Louis was in town Monday.
Go to G. L. Dunn with your prescription. J. M. Gravely of Independence was in town Sunday. Taylor Pershall is again able to be out on the streets. George Vaughn went to Cherryvale last Wednesday. J. M. Henry of Lawrence, Kansas was in the city Monday. Andrew McGuire went down to Independence Wednesday. J. W. Sipple has been appointed umpire for the baseball club. G. L. Dunn and Company handle nothing but sure drugs and medicine. B.S. and Frank McGuire started to Mo. the first of the week. W. E. McGuire and lady went to Arkansas City Monday on a short wedding tour. Nick Kaufman, son of our post master returned home from Kansas City last week. Sipples annd Pershall L.O.L.P. invite you to call and inspect their goods and prices before buying elsewhere. Quick sales and small profits are what suits the purchaser.
Miss Bessie Wells of Coffeyville is in the city visiting John Romick and family this week. Reverend D. J. B. Ross of Havana in Chautauqua with Mr. Finley made us a pleasant call Monday. Some of the boys are pretty good on the diamond. You should drive out some evening and see them. Found on the sidewalk in front of my store last Sunday morning a pocket book containing some money. The owner may have the same by proving property and paying for this ad. James Monroe.

Married: McGuire- Slater Last Monday July 23 at the residence of Mr. Barrett by Rev. D. J. Ross of Havana. Mr. W. E. Mc Guire to Miss Jennie Slater, both of this city. Them parties of both well and favorably known here and the Express joins a host of friends in wishing the happy couple a happy and prosperous journey through life.

August 3, 1888

Adds Local :

Hot, Some sickness, Ice on demand, Choice peaches, Apples plentiful, These be dog days, More new buildings, Monday moving day, Sunday was very sultry, Watermelons are numerous, Milk Shake at Dans, Harshbargers for meats, Keep an eye on the dogs, Sat. was a busy day, Peaches are next in order, Subscribe for the Express, How are your hands boys? Pleasant evenings for a dance, Old paper for sale at this office, Wichita is to have woolen mills. Try the milk shake at Vaughn's, Atchison wants a new depot and wants it bad, The milk shake is the national drink in Kansas, Gasoline got in it's work on two victims at Parsons, There are a great many selfish people in the world , The thermometer went 110 last Sunday in the shade, As these are dog days, keep your eyes open and watch the dog, King men country raises pineapples, eggs, and other tropical fruits, The grumblers grumbles most when he finds nothing to grumble about, The present is the best 'general purpose' year that Kansas has ever known, it is simply impossible to lie about the millet or corn in Kansas this year.

8-3-1888

Newton girls are afraid of chiggers and do not leave their houses after dark. Lawrence is the Athens of Kansas but the editors fight there just the same as they do in Wichita.* There are 988 children of school age at Great Bend and a new school house will have to be built to hold them. * Soon be fall-dry and hot*August is at hand,* Read Amel's new ad-*Joe Hooker of Cana was in town last Tuesday,*J. B. Koonce of Sedan was in city yesterday,* S. E. Booth of Moline was in the city Wed.,* R. J. Hill of Indy was in town Tues. * Max Taterka of the Agency was in town Friday last,* Thos.P. Smith of Pawhuska was in town Tuesday,*Will Smith of Independence was in town Tuesday,* T. J. Woodward of Saint Louis was in town Wendsday,* Charles A. Wells of Coffeyville was in the city Tuesday,* T. H. Plant of Independence last Monday,* Dr. Kennedy of the Agency was in metropolis yesterday, *J.E. Baker sent to Independence for some fine creamy butter,* John Romick wants to know why he can't put a man out on first, * Jennie Brown of Peru registered at the Chautauqua House last Friday,* James Monroe went to Independence yesterday with two car loads of wheat, * B. H. Dixon of Ark City was in this future metropolis last Wed.* Reverend Ransburg of Fall River preached at the school house last Monday night,* Yesterday a youngster appeared at the residence of T. J. Johnson and demanded shelter and protection. He was taken in of course and Mr.

Johnson says he will always be a democrat. *W. Lewis of Osage Agency was in the future metropolis last Monday.

8-10-1888

*Hot days, *Baseballs is all the rage, * More rain than corn, * ZThe mercury is on top, * Some sickness prevails, * Lots of hay being put up, *New goods daily arriving, * Big times in the Territory, * Watermelons getting larger<* Trade with those who advertise, * The melon is decreasing in price, * Look through the paper carefully, * What a glorious show Friday night last.,* Our merchants report trade is improving, * The candidates are slow in announcing.

Chautauqua House   J. C. Romick, prop.
This house has been refitted and refurnished throughout. Everything neat and clean. Traveling guests will find pleasant entertainment. Coolest and most pleasant rooms in Southern Kansas.
Good Sample Rooms.

Commercial Hotel. First Class $1.00 per day house. Good clean beds and rooms and table furnished with the best the market affords.

C. C. Purcells Brokers Office

Monroe and Company- Groceries, Flour, Canned Goods, Provisions, Cigars, Tobaccos and Coffee.

The 5th. Annual Fair of the Chautauqua County Joint Fair Ass. Will be held at Chautauqua Springs, Kansas, Sept. 9-10-11-12-13- and 14, 1888. Liberal Premiums Competition-Unrestricted-Good Music- Good Speakers.

Full Blood Indian Race and War Dance. The officer and manager of the fair are wide awake and are preparing for a Grand Exhibition and Splendid Time.

Low Rate Rail Road –Let everyone turn out, rest from their labors and cares. Congratulate the members of the society and encourage their

efforts to elevate agriculture, the bases of all Mechanical, Industrial, and Commercial Prosperity.
Admission: Adults 25c   Children 15c

J. P. Pershall   President, Lew Lynn   Secrstary

Real Estate and Exchange Agents: --We have a large list of improved Farms, Raw Lands, Stock Ranches, for Sale and Trade. Merchandise to exchange for lands. We control the choicest of city property and will sell the same on easy terms. Office on Main Street, Chautauqua Springs, Kansas

B. F. Barrett- Boots and Shoes!
I have the best assortment of Boots and Shoes in Southern Kansas which I am selling at Bed Rock Prices for Spot Cash. Call and inspect my stock.

Big Bargains in Linen, Alapack, and Seersucker. Coats and Vests, Dusters and for both men and boys.
Summer Underwear, Lawns, Fina Dress Goods, Hose, Straw Hats, and so forth.
We are giving great Bargains in these goods and it is to your interest to call in and see us at once. Men's and Boys ready made clothing, Hats,Shoes, and so forth. Are also going at bargains. Groceries and Provisions also   at great at great bargains. Call and see us. McGuire Brothers.

Chautauqua Mineral Springs Bath House
Stephen Johnson Prop. Hot or cold baths 25 Electric baths 50c
Chautauqua Springs, Kansas
8-10-1888

Directory City of CQ   CQ Co Joint Stock—Fair Assoc. Me Church-UB Church—Union SS, CQ GAR—Chosen Friends Lodge—RR Time Table

Our Farmers say their corn stands so thick on the ground that chickens driven into the field at midday will immediatly go to roost.

Additional local—*Hot days, *Baseball is the rage* More rain more corn,* some sickness prevails, * Lots of hay being put up,* New goods daily arriving,* Big time in the Territory, *Watermelon getting larger,* Trade with those who advertise,* The melon is decreasing in price,* Look through the paper carefully, * What a glorious show Friday night last,* One merchant report trades improving-*The Candidates are slow in announcing. * Lunch and Ice Cream Parlor—George VaughnProp. I also carry a full line of Candies, Nuts, Canned Goods, Cigars, Tobaccos, Nuts, Canned Goods, Cigars, Tobaccos, and Pop. 3rd door South of Post Office, Chautauqua, Kan.

Livery, Feed, Exchange, and Sale Stables. I. E. Imel Prop. Good rigs and saddles and horses.

Chautauqua House   J. C. Romick Prop

T. J. Dunn and Son
Physicians and Surgeons- A full line of drugs and chemicals
Office on west side of Main Street.

Furniture and Undertaker-- T. J. Johnson, Prop.

The Elephant Livery Stable—Good rigs, good saddle horses furnished at the most reasonable prices.
We run a Daily Hack to and from the Osage Agency, Indian Territory.
Share of your patronage solicited.
Clotfelter and Booth prop.

J. N. Goff dealer in Harness- Saddles-Bridles-, Whips-, Collars,- Robes,- Brushes,- Whips,- Collars,_ Robes,_ and in fact everything usually kept in a first class Harness Shop. Repairing neatly done.

There is a clergyman in England named Straight whose curate is named Crooked.

Christie Murray the English novalist is about to publish a volume of poems.

Harvard has made Secretary Fairchild an L.L.D. Daniel Lamont still remains an M. A.

During last year 11,000 pupils in 55 colored schools received aid from the State fund amounting to $45,000.00.

A wire walker with a circus fell 45 feet while performing in a Mass. Town but alighted on his feet and was not hurt.

The salary of the Chief Justice of the Supreme Court is only $10,500.00 A year while a New York judge draws $17,000.00 a year.

A recent census shows one hundred and eightteen factories in operation in the State of North Carolina with a capitol of $1,512,000.00.

Granting marriage license by telephone is the latest development in this scientific age (1888) Bueyrus,O, is the place that deserved the honor of having just made the experiment.

Sipple and Pershall- Dry Goods, Drugs, Medicines, Chemicales, and Oils. Chautauqua, Kansas

Lew Lynn-   Notary Public and Justice of Peace. Office East side of Main Street.
J.E. Baker- dealer in Groceries, Flour, Cigars, Tobacco, Cigars,

Local Happenings:

 *Grain report- buying report business is fair.
*Lew Lynn went to Sedan Tues. last.
*Still the work on the church progresses..
*R. B. Miller of Kansas City was in town Sunday.
*D. E. Wassom of Independence was in town Tues.
*C. W. Ewing and lady of Sedan was in town last Sat.
*What a glorious rain visited this section last Monday night.
*You can see a wonderful change in the corn since the rains.
*We would like to know what has become of the city council.
*Fred L. Bowles of Washington D. C. was in the city Sat.
*James Monroe shipped another car of wheat to Texas tis week.

*Charles Dunmore lost a fine gold watch between here and Sedan last Monday.

*A man may play the winning cards all through life but Gabriel will play the last trump!

*C. E. Brown and lady of Havana came over Frid. A.m. in a buggy to attend a picnic.

*L.R. Darby of Independence was in the city last Frid. And it is needless to say that he took in the picnic.

*George Vaughn's new building is looming up like a tower on a hill and ere long will be ready to occupy.

*John Slater of Elk City has been in the city for a few days visiting his brother I.E. Imel and family.

*There is talk of an excursion from Longton to Elk City to Chautauqua Springs in the near future. Elk City Eagle.

*The person who last their pipe can have the same by calling at this office and paying for this notice.

*William Charles, Division of Road master of the Chicago, Kansas, and Western Railroad was in the city Friday last taking in the sights.

*W. R. Scott and lady of Independence were in the city taking in the sights Friday night last.

*Miss Bessie Wells of Coffeyville who has been visiting in the city for two weeks past returned home the later part of last week.

*Owing to a new mail message on the train our mail was thrown off at Peru at which place it remained until Wed. night.

*Our base ball club has an invitation to go to Peru on the 23rd. and play the Sedan club another game. What do you say boys? We can't do any worse than we did here.

*One of George Jones little boys while handling a target rifle last month accidentally discharged, the bullet taking effect in his left hand inflicting a painful wound.

*Frank McGuire who went to Mo. a short time ago returned the first of the week. It may possibly be that Frank was anxious to return to the health giving Springs.

*Havana is to have a baseball club in the near future. The club will

*probably be here to compete for the $50.00 premium offered by our Fair Association on the champion base ball club.

There will probably be a number of the baseball clubs here to compete for the prize on the 13th. of Sept.

In a marriage one and one make one. In a divorce one from one leaves two.

If the eyes are the windows of the soul it is fair to assume that the lids are the shutters.

A woman with two tongues has been discovered in Alabama. She became a widow at a very tender way.

August 17, 1888

*peaches are plentiful. * Fall goods arriving *The farmer is happy *Summer almost ended* Peaches $1.00 a bushel* Count fair not far off. *A bad dollar in circulation. *The weather continues warm *Water melons large and cheap. * Who went to Sedan to play ball? *Camp meeting days approaching. * Dog days will end the 26th of this month. *August is general considered a long month. * These evenings are just elegant for star gazing. * The Delinquent tax list in the Times Journal looms up.* The general run of prophets predict that August will be a hot month.* The young man who wants to get up with the sun must not sit up too late with the daughter. * You can tell when a dog is warm the same as you can tell a dude when you meet him on the street by his loud pants. * We will give The Express free for one year to a person bringing us the heaviest dozen of sweet potatoes or beets between now and Oct. 1. * An ear of Kansas corn, it is said, fallen across the public road it completely shuts off travel on the road until it can be removed or a new road built.
Chautauqua House   j. C. Romaic prop.

T. J. Dunn and Son   Physician and Surgeon

Furniture and Undertaker   T. J. Johnson

The Elephant Livery Stable   Clotfelter and Booth

Comm Hotel   J. E. Baker

C. C. Purcell's   Brokers Office

8-17-1888 W. J. Wright

Local Happenings

*New corn in the market.

*Dr. Hawkins was in Sedan Wed.

*Lew Lynn went to the hub Wed.

* Rev. Browning was at Peru last week.

* Stephen Johnson is on the sick list this week.

* Considerable sickness prevails in this vacinity.

*Who were the serenders last Sat. night.

* Will Lane of Elgin was in the city yesterday.

*J. Y. Finley of Cherryvale was in town Tues.

* M. L. Jackson of Sedan was in town yesterday.

* W. S. Fitzpatrick of Sedan was in town Saturday.

*Rev. Bryant of Cedar Vale was in town Tues.

*John A. Regan of Osage Agency was in town Tue.

* Fall is rapidly pushing forward and soon be here.

* Remember the dates of the fair-Sept. 11, 12, 13, and 14.

* We printed 500 sale bills for Sipple and Pershall this week.

* Tom Cocannon went down to Independence yesterday.

* The work on Vaughns new building is progressing nicely.

* George Edwards went down to Independence Wed.

* Ed Brunt of Osage Agency was in the city Wed.

* The well drillers are now engaged in sinking a well at Glovers.

*Watermelons sell now days for 5c and nice ones at that

* Judge Pettit and son of Osage Agency was in town Sat.

* Will Scott of Independence was doing our merchants Wed.

* Mrs. W. S. Browning has been on the sick list during the past week.

* Quite a number of our citizens were in Sedan the first of the week.

* C. A. Clotfelter of Cherryvale was in the city Monday last on business.

*Mrs. Alldredge is lying seriously ill at her home in the south part of the city.

- H. S. Wilhelm of Coffeyville was in the city Thursday looking after his log business.
- Miss E. Prilliman of Sedan registered at the Chautauqua House Sat.
- Comcannon went down to the territory Wed. to take a number of views of farms, ranches, and so forth.

- Base ball practice this evening at the fair ground.
- All members of the club are requested to come out.
- J. L. Stallard had his house removed from the rear of the depot to his lot on the corner just west of the lumber yard.
- William Charles of Cherryvale, the rustling division roadmaster of the Southern Kansas Rail Road was in town Tues.
- E. R. Bennett was out nearly all last week putting up and distributing fair bills and handing out premiums lists for the coming fall fair.
- Born to Mr. and Mrs. I. E. Imel of this city on Monday night August 13, a bouncing baby girl.
- Mrs. C. A. Clotfelter of Cherryvale and Mrs. James Lynch of Cedar Vale sisters of Rev. W. S. Browning of this city are here visiting this week.
- The girl who can put a good square patch on a pair of pantaloons may not be accomplished as one who can embroider and work green worsted on blue ground but will be far more useful at the head of a large family.
- The Vanderbuilts' spend enormous sums on furniture, bric-brac and artistic decorations but comparatively little on jewelry.
- It is said that there are farmers wives of Long Island who make boys trousers for 3 cents.
- There are women in New York who toil 16 hours a day for 60 cents.
- Mrs. Dr. Smith has contributed $12,000.00 for the purpose of constructing a play house for the use of the children of Newark, New Jersey who have no place but the streets to play in.
- All the sporting of the east are now agreed that John F. Sullivan is a dead duck in the pond. His brutally aided by whiskey has driven away friends and wrecked his health.
- A Mexican paper declares that the American Nation will never amount to anything until it takes up bull fighting as a national sport. It needs such plain talk as that to take the conceit out of us.
- The "worst blizzard of the season" has been changed to "The worst thunderstorm of the year"
- The Fire Engine horses of Montgomery Alabama must be driven to a fire at a slow trot. This gives crippled and old folks a chance to get out of the way.

8-24-1888

*Katy dids. *After harvest.* Decreasing daylight. * Summer is flitting by. * Fall will soon be here. * Rail Road travel is brisk. * Grapes are in the market. * Peaches and cream soon. Sunday was a gloomy day. * There will be lots of apples. *Candidates are coming forth. * These are beautiful evenings for driving . * We shall soon have the beautiful evenings for driving. *We shall soon have the beautiful autumn season. *Our merchants report business improving. * The doctors report less sickness since the recent rains and warm weather. *The present month has 5 Wednesdays and 5 Thursdays and 5 Fridays.

Local Happenings

*Farmers all happy-Kansas is in luck this year-Soon be camp meeting days-These evenings are just simply elegant- New corn finds a ready market at a fair price-C. C. Purcell went to Independence yesterday- E. L. Holt of Kansas City was in town Monday-N. W. Terry of St. Louis was in the city Monday._ Strangers are numerous on our streets now a days.-This week has afforded some fine nights for sleeping.—W.P. Brown of Cherryvale was in town Wednesday.-The time set for the big fair is rapidly approaching.-R. P. Evans of Kansas City was in town Monday last.-W. J. McPhee of Kansas City was in town Monday last. Send the Express to your friends and escape letter writing.-James Ridgeway of Columbus , Ohio was in town Monday. —W. T. White of Lawrence, Kansas was in the city last Monday.- William Macbee of Sedalia, Mo. was in the city last Monday.-J.C. Armstrong of Ark City was in the city last Saturday. Francis M. Stine of Marshall, Mo. was in the city Mon.-Jake Kaufman went to Cedar Vale last. Monday evening on special business. D. V. Hereford of Kansas City was perambulating our streets last Monday. E. M. Mathews the rustling Marshall of Pawhuska was in the city Sat.—James A. Vawter shipped several boxes of choice peaches to Ottawa the first of the week.   The ball game Sat. between the Chautauqua and Havana clubs promises to be an interesting one.=Hi Woodring, the rustling grain buyer of Elk City was in the city last Monday and Tuesday on business.

--To make t town lively patronize it's merchants and laborers. Don't spend a cent away from home that can't be spent here. --The largest camp meeting ever held in the county will commence here on September 15th and continue the remainder of the month.
Every body cordially invited. J. L. Stallard will soon open a meat market in his building just west of the lumber yard where he will keep constantly on hand a full supply of choice meats. –J. R. Skinner an extensive trader of the Osage Agency who has been visiting in St. Louis, Washington, and several other eastern cities for a number of weeks –returned home last Tuesday.—Chautauqua against Havana will play Sat. in Chautauqua.

8-31-1888

Add Local:
More rain-Somewhat cooler—Peaches are small—Fall close at hand—Summer almost ended—Autumn almost here—Days growing shorter—

Nights getting longer—School will soon commence—Water melons are holding on—Peaches on market at 50c.-Leap year is sadly on the wane—Lots of people in town Sat.-Kansas is a lucky state this year,-- a delightful shower Sunday morning—Fall grass promises an abundant crop, - The summer will soon have faded away—Dog days are over and hot weather soon will be—August is usually the dullest month of the year, This is the fifth issue of the Express in this month,-Melons are wholesome if you don't burrow into the rind. We are commencing to have a taste of those perfect days—The Shades of night are fast colors. The finest grapes ever raised in any country are now coming to market.
The evenings are full of sounds. The crickets and katydids predominating. There will be a cyclone of brass band music during the autumn months. The barns are full—so is the farmer of thankfulness. At least he ought to be—The time will soon be here when the question of filling the coal bins will agitate our people. Day light is growing less every day. If there ever was a season that deserves a big harvest home it is the one that occurred in 1888.

It pays and looks better to make the surrounding s of your home dwelling attractive even if you are a renter.

It is now conceded that the corn crop of Kansas will be fully 200,000,000 bushels. This at 30c per bushel will amount to $60,000,000.00. The gross value of corn, wheat, and oats in this state will be about $90,000,000.00.

Chautauqua House   J. C. Romick
T. J. Dunn and Son   Physicians and Surgeons
Furniture and Undertaker   T J. Johnson
The Elephant Livery Stable   Clotfelter and Booth
Harness and Saddles   J. N. Goff

One of the richest men in Saint Paul who owns block after block of real estate lives on less than $800.00 per year.

Mrs. Booth of Washington County, Tenn. died recently in the log house she was born in 98 years ago. She had in all that time never been further than 5 miles from home.

A colored man near Macon, Ga. Has committed to memory the entire Holy Bible. A few years ago he could not read and claims that his knowledge has been revealed to him in a vision.

Numerous cases of diarrhea have been traced by Dr. L. W. Sedwick to the use of fruit from tin cans. Such fruits invariably contained salts of tin which have been hither to suppose to be harmless.

Carson, Nevada reports an acrolite weighing ten tons that is streaked with horn silver and which fell upon a race course, narrowly missing a jockey who was exercising a colt there at the time.

Justice Charles at Liverpool recently sentenced a man to 7 years penal servitude and his wife to the same punishment for life for cruelty to their child, a little girl whom they had kept imprisoned in a dark cellar and had beaten, burned with a hot poker, and other wise abused.

A Railway employee in Vienna who had just been sentenced to six months imprisonment for ill treating his wife drew a revolver from his pocket and shot at random into the audience wounding one person. Then he shot himself in the head and will probably die. The police officials who failed to search him properly will be disciplined.

Watermelons are legal tender in this section now, They are the kind of greenbacks that few object to.

The hay crop is excellent this year and the late rains are still adding to the crop. There will be no scarcity this coming winter of stock feed.

We have read the perineum list of the Caney Valley Fair Association, Granola, Kansas. The fair will be held September 26, 27, 28, and 29, 1888. We also acknowledge receite of complimentary sent us by the offices.

Do Chinch bugs lay eggs? Is a question that seems to agitate the Kansas farmer. If they do and are as bad as the hen's eggs that come into market in warm weather there will be but little danger of one in a million hatching.

Local Happenings   8-31-1888

*What did you buy at the sale last month?
*Chautauqua now sports two baseball clubs.
*H. H. Perry of Elgin was in the city Mon.
*W. F. Rodimel of Sedan was in town Mon.
*B. E. Adams of Sedan was in town Mon.
* George Vaughn went to Indy Tuesday.
*A Mr. Fitzpatrick of Sedan was in town Monday.
*There was a large crowd at the sale last Monday.
*J. N. Hodges of Kansas City was in town Sat.
*Watch our columns for a big ad from Kansas City.
* Will Scott of Independence was in town Wed.
* R. B. Cooke and lady of Sedan was in town Frid.
* S. G. Samson of Coffeyville was in town last Frid.
*T. H. Plant of Independence was in town last Mon.
*W. G. Shelton of St. Louis was in town Mon.
*Harris Beemer of Osage Agency was in town Mon.

* W.T. and Thos Leahy of Elgin was in town Mon.

*W. M. Wade of Independence was in town last Frid.

* G. W. Simcox of Osage Agency was in town last Frid.

* E. S. Peckham and lady of Winfield was in town Frid.

*Frank Purcell, the log man, was in town a few days this week.

*Harris Beemer of Osage Agency was in town Sat. last.

*Base ball game at Sedan-today, Highland Center against Sedan.

*Mrs. Wawan of Coffeyville is visiting Mrs. J. C. Romick.

* Call at Mrs. Lees on Bennet's corner for Millinery Goods.

* Miss M. V. McCarthy of Osage Agency was in town Sunday.

* Woster Petitt and son of Osage Agency was in town Monday.

* Candidates were quite numerous   and conspicious last month.

* Ed Tinker of Cana, Osage Nation, was in town last Monday.

*. Price of Peru was in town last Monday attending a sale.

* The quary is, how much did E. R. Bennett pay for his race horse?

* Hotel Chautauqua has had a good run of customers the past two
   weeks.

*M. S. Wilhelm of Coffeyville is in town looking after his log
   interests.

*Mother De Sales and two sisters of Osage Agency have gone to
   Philadelphia and will return next week.

*Remember that we do job printing as cheap as the cheapest and
   first class style. Leave us your order.

*W. F. Sams, candidate for the nomination of clerk of the district
   court by the Republican party was a pleasant caller last month.

* The Chautauqua County Teacher's Association will be held in this
   city Sat. September 14th. instead of September 1 as it was 1st. ann.

*All parties having accounts with us which are past due must call
   and settle at once and save trouble. Long Bell Lumber Company.

*The day on which the Union Labor speaking at the fair is set for
   Thurs. Sept. 13th. The Dems and Republicans will select their days
   to speak soon.

*Today we will remove our office into the building recently vacated
   by George Vaughn. We will occupy the 3 rooms on the north side
   while George Vaughn will occupy the two on the south.

*Charles A. McBrian and Charles Moore of Sedan base ball club
   came over last Sat. to witness the game between our home club and
   the Havana nine but were disappointed as the Havana club failed to
   put in it's appearance

*Mrs. Rub and daughter of Arkansas City returned to their home last Wed. after two weeks visit at our Medical Spring. They expressed themselves as being greatly healed by the usage of these wonderful Medical Waters and can most heartily recommend them all.

*Ed Matthews last Sat. night arrested a man by the name of LOW who escaped from the Winfield jail some two weeks ago who is charged with Horse Theft.

*J. C. Armstrong and his family of Arkansas City have returned home after a week's visit at our Medical Springs. They are highly pleased with the Springs and express themselves as much benefited by use of the Medical Water.

*The Treasurer of Rawlins county, Kansas has decamped for Canada with $10,000.00 of the peoples money.

*The farmers among the Sand Hills of Western Kansas are in poor condition for winter. Their crops are a failure and doubtless aid will be asked before spring.

Sept. 8, 1888

Add Local:

Fine weather—Summer has flown—Pastures are superb—Bountiful harvest returns—Ague will soon be on deck—Potatoes are getting scarcer—Still the water melons roll in—Wheat continues to advance—School commenced Mon.—The Shadows are lengthening.—Clean up around your residence—Some of the choicest of peaches are coming to town—Vacation days are rapidly drawing to a close—Katy dids and crickets now hold nightly concerts—What are you going to to take or send to the fair?—Chinch bugs have done but little damage this year –Fall is on deck and indications promise a lively one.—Squirrels are said to be numerous throughout the timber—There is some sickness among the children of the country.—Call on Mrs. Lee's on Bennetts corner for Millinert needs—Never write the word "finis" backwards, it will be "sin if" do.—The mosquito is a much abused insect-most every body has a slap at him—There's a comet approaching but it will not be visible for some weeks to come—Kansas out to feel her oats, she has 51,000,000 bushels of them this year—The tramp has reached the hay day of his life when he is allowed to sleep in the barn—At this season of the year an ounce of caution at the table is worth a pound of pills in bed—A piece of tallow wrapped in tissue paper and laid among furs or woolen will prevent the ravage of moths—This is a great year for hay in Kansas –The farmers will find it to their interests to harvest as much of it as possible.

Fact or Fancy

The Sioux Indians still refuse to sign the supposed treaty.—Russian eggs are selling in London markets at 6c a dozen.—The July outpost of Lake Superior copper mines amounted to 3,517 tons—The 22 vessels of the new navy will require 5,851 men to equip them—Memphis is the greatest inland cotton market in the world recieving from 700,000 to 1000,000 bales yearly—Middle Tenn has shipped $700,000 worth of new potatoes to northern markets this season already—It is stated that over 500,000 roe plants are annually imported to America from England, France, and Holland—Exports from U. S. amounted to $311,063,639 which is 19,000,000 less then the smallest and $7,000,000 less then the corresponding period of any year of the decade.

Local Happenings   Sept 7, 1888

Don't forget the fair—How is this for autumn?—Fall goods will soon begin to roll in—The city council meets again next evening---The city presented quite a scene last Sat. John Stallard is acting as Street Commissioner—Joe Roberts of Caney was in town Wed.—Frank Cross of Elk City was in town Sat.—S. E. Booth of Moline was in town Wed.—The street commissioner is working on the streets—Joe Futhey of Havana was in town last Tues.—Paul Albert of Pawhuska was in town Sat.—Frank Aiken of Pawhuska was in town Sat.—A good many happy red men in town last Sat. –J. F. Gould of Pawhuska was in town last Sat.—M. Sewell of Independence was in town Wed. – H. J. Hulmer of Detroit Michigan was in town Mon. Matt Miller of Independence was in town Mon.—George Vaughn went down to Independence Tues.—A. L. Chouteau of Pawhuska was in town Sat.—W. Louis of Osage Agency was in town Sat.— Louis Delorer of Pawhuska was in town Wed. A new photograph gallery is located north of our office.—Charles Vaughn made a trip down to Independence last Tues.—McGuire Brothers left us an order for 1000 envelopes this week.

About forty persons boarded the train at this place for Wichita last Sat evening. Mr./ Randall of Fayettville, Ark. is in the city this week visiting Mr. Baker and family and family.

Mrs. Fritch is quite sick this week but is thought to be improving.

J. E. Baker and family went down to Independence yesterday to visit friends and attend fair.

Mrs. Ida McGuire has been quite ill for a week past but at this writing we are glad to say that she is much better.

The Sedan band has been engaged to furnish music at the fair here.

There will be 14 to 18 instruments in the band.

Next week is fair week and if the weather will permit it will be a grand success judging from the present indications.

F. H. Hawkins went to Wichita last Tuesday evening in charge of Will Johnson who is under bond for his appearance in court.

Quite a number of people came up from the Nation including several Indians last Sat. and took the train to Wichita where go to attend court.

A Louisville whiskey firm has deluged Kansas with circulars head "If you sell whiskey in Kansas "about 7000 men who have tried it have sent postal cards to the house simply inscribed "You're a Liar!"

Mrs. M. Cross and daughter and Katie Baird of Elk City are stopped at the Chautauqua House. They are here for the benefit of their health. So far they seem to be improving steadily and think that before long they will be able to return to their homes greatly improved in health.

We are truly glad to learn that they are receiving much benefit from the use of these wonderful Medical Waters and it will afford their many friends at Elk City much pleasure to learn of their greatly improved condition.

The Sulton of Turkey has ordered several typewriters for the ladies of his harem who can write in the French language.

Sept. 14, 1888

Additional Locals:

*Heavy dews. *County fair ends today.* Kansas is the hay state this year. *The price of watermelons is on the decline . *Wheat is selling at 78c one day last week. * Our public school started this fall in good shape. *Farmers are preparing to put out a large acreage of wheat this fall. *This is a good time to clean out the fence corners before the weeds go to seeds. Timely action will save much labor in the future. *Action will save much labor in the future. *Broom corn all over the state is said to be an unusually good crop this year. * it is always a profitable crop. *The lease question in the territory has not yet been settled .They will not get much out of this year if it is not settled pretty soon. *

Chautauqua House   J. C. Romick prop.

T. J. Dunn   Physician and Surgeon

Furniture and Undertaker   T. J. Johnson

The Elephant Livery Stable   Clotfelter and Booth

Harness and Saddles   J. N. Goff

Sept. 14, 1888

Local Happenings:

*Autumn weather. *Moonlight nights. *Vacation days are over.
* School children numerous. * What lonely nights to sleep.
* Quite a refreshing shower this afternoon. *The mornings are cool
and refreshing. * David Ellis of Peru was in town yesterday. *Sedan
beats the world record for cranky base ballists. *Quite a number
attends the fair at this place. *T. J. Six of Waverly, Ill. was a caller
Wed. * Business has been exceedingly good this past week. The
Sedan Band make pretty good music, don't you think?
* Elder Ross of Havana was in town Wed. * W. F. Sams of Little
Caney township was in town yesterday. * E. R. Linebough of Sedan
was a pleasant caller last Mon. evening. *Will Lane of Elgin has been
helping Charley Vaughn this week in the barber shop. * We don't
see why Baker and Bennet did not enter their race horses at the fair.
*Tom Concannon returned from Independence Frid. Where he had
been taking views. * Rowden and Family of Chautauqua Springs
have moved into the Sheets property in this city. Havana Herald.
*Mrs. Lee of Chautauqua Springs visited with Mrs. G. W. Brown
this week. Havana Herald. * F. M. Kennesson of Cedar Vale Star
was a pleasant caller at this office. * The Indian race yesterday
evening was quite interesting and was witnessed by a large crowd.
* Wyatt Cranor and lady and Mrs. Menden Hall snd daughter, Miss
Jenny of Havana was attending the fair here yesterday. * Sedan was
surely deserted dring the past week judging from the number of
their people who were attending the fair here this week. *Charles W.
Baird of Elk City was in town last Saturday and of course made this
office a pleasant call. Charles is one of our old school mates. *
Mrs. Finley sent to this office last Mon. evening a fine large sweet
potatoe which weighed 3# and 5oz/ for which she will please accept
our thanks. * Mrs. M. A. Sherfie of McCune, Kansas is in the city
visiting with C. E and G. S. Vaughn and families. She is very
favorably impressed with the appearance of our thriving city.

Sept. 21, 1888

*Mild September. *Wheat on the ground. * Business is thriving.
*Wild plums are ripe. */Hay making. *Strangers are coming in.
*Corn cutting fashionable, * Wheat threshing continues. * The
quinine demand is slow. * Huge stocks of corn in the fields.
*Comfort the sick and help the needy. *Fine haying weather for this
time of year.* Call at this office for Superior Job Printing.
Hunters are beginning to clean their guns. * The plowman
homeward plods his weary way. * The work of putting in wheat has
earnestly begun. *Wild plums have produced in abundance this year.
*The ground is in fine condition for drilling in wheat. * The road to
the highest success is never an easy one. *Sale bills printed with
neatness and dispatch at this office. *The second crop of hay is good
and lots of it is being put up. *The mosquito makes the evening very
uncomfortable with it's buzz and bite.

Last Saturday was another lively day for business men. *Trade is
picking up on every hand.   * Mrs. J. C. Romick and children were
over from Chautauqua Springs last week. * Guests of Mrs. R. L.
Wells of Coffeyville Journal. * County Treasurer Stallard has leased
the Barrington residence and will move into it shortly and be ready
to take pens of the Treasure's office promptly on time.
Times Journal.

*Rev. J. W Scott father in law of candidate Harrison is 90 years of
age. Evangelist Moody advises young men who desire to be
revivalists to start out as book agents and study human nature.

Chautauqua House – J. C. Romick prop.
T. J. Dunn and Son   Physician and Surgeon
Furniture and Undertaker   T. J. prop.
The Elephant Livery Stable Clotfelter and Booth

Princes Christian of England has been induced by the Queen, her
mother, to post pone her intention of joining the Romich Church.

Austin Corbin was born in Keene New Hampshire. Early in life he emigrated to Iowa. He made his first start in life in Western land speculation.

Except that his sandy beard begins to show streaks of gray ex President Rutherford B. Hays shows scarcely a change in the appearance he presented ten years ago.
Grermany's new Emperor is distributing pictures and images of himself broadcast. One of his latest freaks was to have himself photographed beside Bismarck.

Queen Victoria has gained greatly in flesh this summer. When she puts a nice nickel in the slot she realizes that even the sovereign of England may have too much weight in the world.

Mrs. St. Elmo Evans Wilson has bought and decorated a luxurious home near Mobile with the proceeds of her gorgeous novels. She writes in a Chinese pagoda bower in her flower garden.

Reprehensive Amos J. Cummings is the son of a New Jersey preacher and it is said by Washington newspaper that he used to play the fiddle in the orchestra of his father's church when a boy.

Anyone looking for a good location to stop where they can find plenty of feed, a good live town with splendid schools and a good opening for almost any kind of business need look noo farther than our thriving little city for she contains all of them.

9-21-88

A drummer who has been to Cincinnati Centennial reports that he saw the Kansas corn there towering above that of the other States and he heard an old lady remark as she gazed at it "You needn't tell me that corn grew that tall in one year. There's two or three years of growth there!

The oldest pupil now attending school in the United States is past age 60. He is Crazy Head, a former chief of the Crow Nation and is enrolled as a pupil at the Carlisle Indian School.

Real Estate and Exchange Agents   Purcell and Beaston

**Groceries and Flour   canned goods Cigars, Tobaccos
Monroe Bros.**

*George L. Dunn was at Elgin last Tues.

* John Romick has been on sick list this week.

* Will Franks went to Pawhuska this morning.

* John Hays of Elgin was in town Sat. last.

*Andrew McGuire is in the Territory this week.

*Rose Gonshird of Sedan of Sedan was in town Sat.

*Hattie Floyd of Sedan was in town sat.

* Will Lane returned to Elgin last monday evening.

* R. S. Thornburg of Sedan was in town Sat.

*Bell Light of Sedan was in our city Sat. last.

* Our sportmen talk hunting and fishing now a days.

* S. C. Swan of Independence was in town Tues.

* S. E. Booth of Moline was in town last Wed.

*C. A. Clotfelter of Cherryvale was in town Mon.

*8 Harris Brenner of Osage Agency was in town Tues.

* J. Cunningham of Osage was in town Sat.

* C. W. Ewing and lady of Elgin were in town Sat.

*J. W. Wynn and lady of Sedan were in town Sat.

*Frank Cross of Elk City was in town last week.

*G. S. Hartley of Osage was in City Sat.

* Mrs. R. S. Thornburg of Sedan was in city Sat.

* C. D. Murphy of Cincinnati, Ohio Sat.

* D. E. Wassam of Independence was in town Sat.

* W. Wingett of Sioux City, Iowa in city Tues.

*W. T. Shafer reg. at the Chautauqua House Tues.

*E. R. and A. A. Fouts both of Sedan were in city Sat.

* Rev. P. Scott of Independence registered in the CQ House Sat.

*J. E. Warner of Washington D. C. was was perambulating our
 streets Sat.

*A.Y. Buckles of Sedan was in town last week attending the
 teacher's Ass.

*Mrs. J. E. Baker left last Tues. for Fayetteville, Arkansas where she
 has a sister is ill.

*The Sedan Graphic and the Elk City Eagle are trying to see who can say the meanest things about each other.

*See the ad of L. G. Super's, the new shoemaker. Mr. Soper is here to stay and asks your patronage.

*Ed Glover has resigned his position in the Elephant Livery Stable and has accepted a situation as clerk in Edwards grocery store.

Will Johnson who was charged with murder was examined before the US District Court in Wichita last week and was acquitted.

Randall and Oliver have purchased the stock of Dry Goods, Groc. and so forth from A. C. Cadwell and have been invoicing the stock this week.

The freight going to the Agency will be hauled hereafter from Elgin instead of from here the contract being made for the same last Tues.

When prescriptions are compounded by a registered Pharmacist there will be no danger of mistakes and if you want pure drugs in all prescriptions go to Sipple and Pershalls Drug Store.

Mrs. F. J. Fritch who has been dangerously ill for more than a week past is recovering slowly but ere long it is thought that she will be able to be up and around again.

Sipple and Pershall are leaders of low prices in Dry Goods, Clothing, Notions, Boots, and Shoes. They carry nothing but the best goods and sell them for the least money,

Lee McPheron of Sedan was a pleasant caller at this office last Wed. evening.

Mr. McPheron was the first to enter upon journalism in this city and says since he left here the population has entirely changed.

A five year old boy died in Neodesha last week from Hydrophobia.

The Justice and Police court was the center of attraction last Monday a.m. Some 'toughs" from Independence were going to 'learn people something". The way they conducted themselves Sunday night was simply inhuman and the result of their actions they were brought before "Squire Lynn" who gave them a neat little fine including the necessary trimmings which was paid and they were released.

Bargain Column---

Baled hay at Monroe's---A first class lunch at Dunmore's for only 15c.

Pea Berry Coffee at Cadwells'..

For a dish of Fresh Oysters go to George Vaughn's.

George Vaughn's—All parties having accounts which are past due must call and settle at once and save trouble-Long Bell Lumber Co.

For baled hay go to Monroes.

For good cigars, Lemonade, and fresh oysters go to Dunmore's. Stallard's New Meat Market is always supplied with the choicest fresh meats which will always be sold at the lowest prices.

Mrs. Edwards has a large stock of millinery goods of the latest styles has just been received. Call at Mrs. Lees on Bennets' corner for millinery goods.

Go to G. L. Dunn and Cc with your prescription.

One set of Harness free. I will make the person a present who buys the greatest number of cigars and Blossom, Honost John, or Special Drive brands within the next 60 days, of a handsome set of single driving harness. George Vaughn.

Cattle are dying in considerable numbers on Grand River I T.

The largest woman in the country died last week: she weighed 849 pounds.

An immense wheat crop and an enormas corn crop and a big hay crop in this vicinity assures the farmers a profitable year.

Only four months longer of lrap year and marriage licenses seem to be a drug on the market. The girls don't seem to want to marry as bad as the boys thought they did.

According to an exchange Kentucky has 6 counties: Harlan, Knot, Perry, Letcher, Bell, and Leslie that have never had a church within their borders during the sixty or seventy years of their existence as counties. How much differently our Kansas people are- a church in every little village in the State.

Livery, Feed, Exchange and Sale Stable. I. E. Imel, prop.

Entered the Post office at Chautauqua, Kansas as Second Class mail matter.

J. B. Beaston   City Auctioneer

J. E. Baker   Groceries and Flour

September 28, 1888
Additions:

Look after the filthy hog pen about now.
Get in your winter coal before the price goes up .
Hunters are improving their time and young chickens must suffer.
The oyster epicure always takes the first of the season the half shell.
Disease lurks in dreadful quantizes in the neglected out houses.
Ladies, Leap Year is fast passing away. Don't neglect your opportunity.
There are more than 4000 people in the United States who are over 100 years of age.

In the life of a maiden as well as in a thermometer 32 degrees is the freezing (out) point.

Someone says that wealth is a shadow . This is why we are advised to secure the shadow ere the substance fades.

People who go away for time this season of the year all return confirmed in the belief that there is no place like home.

They have a method of implanting natural teeth but in a matter of brains a man must worry along with his original supply.

An immense amount of hay has been put up this fall in Chautauqua County as compared with the crops of any previous year. It is well.

The Indian Territory owing to the absence of first during hatching season this year is reported to be fairly alive with Quails, Pheasants, and Prairie Chickens as a support of the human race Corn is not kind: That small white grain known as rice is the Monarch of the foods. It is believed to support a larger number of the human race than any other grain.

9-28-88

A state bought by the price of so much human blood, blest with lovely climate and deep rich soil can not be otherwise than grand. Kansas is such a country, thus her phenomenal growth. In 1890 she will have two million people.

In 1861 England imported 150,000,000 pounds of wool and 615,000,000 pounds of wool two years ago.

We receive 17,000,000 pounds of cocoanuts per year from Central America. In rainy weather the trees shed in three days and every two days on fair days. They average about 180 nuts per year.

William Scully, alias 'Lord Scully' the alien Illinoisan land lord will offer his farms for sale and dispose of all of his property in the states. By enforcement of lien land law, Scully's system of 'rack renting' has been broken up, his tenants refusing to pay.

Capturing grasshoppers is now a favorite occupation in some parts of Minnesota. The popular method of capture is to cover the inner arc of a wheeled wire toothed rake with cotton cloth and drive where the grass hoppers are the thickest. In a short time a few bushels of the pests are collected on the cloth.

They are Tabooed! It is understood that the following pledge will be circled for signature among the journalists of the daily press. "I hereby solemnly promise that I will never use the following expectations or of them in my professional work and that I will use honorable means to prevent the use of them by others.

"Fire Friend"—"Cast of Gloom" –"When the smoke of battle had cleared away "---The scene beggars description View with alarm" –Sickening thud" "Like the play of Hamlet with Hamlet left out" "Trembled like   an aspen" Lap of Luxury" Hive of industry" "White winged peace" Fill a long felt want" Hectic flush" "Grim Reaper"   "Throw oil on the troubled waters"+

Sign here---------------.

There are over a million dollars worth of Fairbanks scales sols in 1887

The Masons of Missouri have been asked to contribute to the yellow fever suffers.

Fredonia's water works are completed and the citizens say their reservoir has hardly an equal in the state.

Note Lost! A note for the amount $369.00 from John Ferrell, Mose Shaw, Robert Houx and Thomes Henderson dated March 12, 1888 due 5 months after date payable to McGuire Brothers is lost. The above reasons are hereby notified not to pay said note unless presented by the proper owners, McGuire Brothers. The finder of said note will please leave the same at our place of business. McGuire Brothers.

Local Happenings:

Mrs. Pershall was quite ill last week.
Mrs. Hilton has been quite sick this week.

J. Prunish of Sedan was in town last Sunday night.

Will Rodimel of Sedan was in town last Sunay.

C. W. Baird of Elk City was in town last Friday.

J. E. Baker went down to Agency Monday.

J. M. Roger of Kansas City was in town Sat.

S. W. Moon of Chicago   was in town Sat.

A load of onions found a ready market Wed.

H. R, Brooks of Havana was in the city Frid.

H. B. Kelley of Independence was in the city Mon.

C. H. Burnes of Lawrence was in town Sat.

W. N. Anderson of Cedar Vale was in town Sun.

Will Scott of Independence was in town Wed.

Will Lane has put in a barber chair at the bath house.

John Frazier was over from Havana Sat.

I. H. Hamilton of Kansas City was in town Sat.

H. W. Feig of S. K. R. R. was in town Sun.

Read Dr. Woolsey's card to be found in this issue.

Jake Kaufman and Tom ConCannon went to Sedan yesterday.

George Thrasher- The new Havana deliveryman was in town Last Sat.

Have you left your measure at the new shoe shop for a pair of boots or shoes?

Miss Edmonden of Sedan was in the city Sunday at the camp meeting.

Ed Oliver and Mr. Fairbanks made a trip to Independence Tues. last.

A large number of Peru folks were attending the camp meeting at this place Sunday.

Randall and Oliver have erected a warehouse on the rear of the store room.

Miss Gertie Rowden formerly of this city but now of Havana is visiting in this city this week.

During the day the camp meeting has not been very well attended but at night the crowd is larger.

Remember that if you ride or drive across the side walk   you are subject to a fine not less than $1.00 nor more than $25.00.

J. J. Holden called at this office last Wed. and made us glad by flashing up a dollar and a half for some job work.

Mrs. Cross and daughter Mrs. Katie Baird who have been here for some weeks past for their Health returned to Elk City on short visit last Friday morning.

Bargain Column:-Baled Hay at Monroe's.

A first class lunch at Dunmore's for only 15c.

For a dish of fresh oysters go to George Vaughn's.

For baled hay go to Monroe's.

Oct. 5, 1888

Add Local:

Cool nights.-Chilly wind.-Apples are plentiful.-Clean out your premises.-Fall wheat is about all sowed,-Corn husking is the order of the day.-McPherson is cursed with "Till Tappers". It is about time for the fall crop of weddings.- Buy your winter fuel while it is cheap.- Diphtheria is prevalent in some   of the Atchison schools. Clay Center has just dedicated a new Episcopal Church.

Kansas apples are said to be much better this year. The Katydid and cricket continue to rasp out their nocturnal strains.

Trego County boys hunt water melon patches with shot guns and club the old farmers that object. Prat City is to have an electric light system and a company has been organized there for that purpose.-Wyandotte man's cellar was entered the other night and robbed of every thing eatable and drinkable.==A full grown young and a 13 year old girl of diminutive proportions were married near this city on Sunday evening. Judge Brown refused the license until the mother and a sister of the child joined in application.—Coffeyville Journal.

10-5-1888

The highest price paid in cash for eggs and butter and drakes located in Bennet's building.

The council met Monday night.

Mrs. Friitch is still quite ill.

Tom Concannon has gone to the Agency.

A. Nelson of Osage was in town Sat.

Mrs. Hilton is again able to be up and around.

Dr. Kennedy of the Agency was in town Mon.

J. H. Beatty of Jonesburg was in last Wed.

J.C. Barnes of Kansas City was in town Frid.

C. C. Percell went to Lamar, Mo. Wed. am

W. A. Ferguson of St. Louis was in city Frid. Last

H. H. Broom of Independence was in town Sun.

Ye Scribe visited at Havana last Sun.

Andrew Mc Guire was down to Independence Tues.

Horace P. Debble of Kansas City was in town Sundat.

J. M. Carpenter of Pawhuska was in town Sat.

Hi Woodring of Elk City was in town several days last week.

G. S. Hartley and family of Pawhuska was in town Friday last.

James Monroe made a trip over to Havana and Caney last week.

Frank Croons of Elk City spent several days in the city.

Mr. Hilton came up from the Nation Sat and spent Sunday with his family.

The Grenola Chief has turned a new leaf and now preaches the Union Labor Doctrine to it's readers.

It will soon be time to put up the heating stove. Do not let your angry passions rise if the pipe does not fit at first.

Willie Johnson and Bruce Finley have gone to La Compton to attend school.

We understand that the Independence and Sedan ball clubs will cross bats at Independence soon. We thought the Sedan boys knew more thaan to tackle the Independence Club again.

The largest sweet potatoe we have seen this year was raised by J. W. Shawl which weighed when first taken from the ground a fraction over 8#s Step into Lew Lynns office to look at it.

While at the depot the other evening W. A. Higgins button left his team standing unhitched at his surprise, returning to where he had left them, saw them going to town at break neck speed. The wagon was loaded with barb wire which was scattered all over the road, the box was thrown off, the tongue broken, and more or less damage done.

Died: Mrs. John Davis died at her residence at Jonesburg, Kansas Monday Oct. 1, 1888. Ike Beaston died at his home last Monday 10th.

Mrs. Alexander, mother of J. W. Alexander died at her home last Thursday.

10-12-1888

Add Local

The stupid flies. –Fine fall weather.-Cool and pleasant.—The wheat is aall sewed.—Send your children to schoo.—Only four weeks till the great election.—Apples are still coming to town in abundance.—Leap Year is fast coming close but the young ladies don't seem to worry much about it.—Life in Kansas is becoming sweeter every day.—Owing to the number of sugar factories in operation with such bountiful crops our people   should feel the happiest and most contented of any people under the sun....—The wheat market has gone up more in the last few days than it had in thr past 5 years.—That's what the farmers wants. Theodore Stout and his wife of Sulphur Springs, Arkansas are visiting friends in Sedan this week.—Governor Guy Marched into the capitol of the Chickasaw Nation one day last week and took his seat. It seems he was legally elected but was cemented out by the Byrd Party. Trouble is anticipated.

Local Happenings:
A light shower Tuesday night.—Fire in the mornings are agreeable.—Alex Bryan was at Conference—Read Kaufman's new confectionary.—Notice the new Feed store sign.--
N. Neff of Detroit, Michigan was in town Sunday'
C. A. McBrian of Sedan was in town Sun.
Dr. Dalby of Jonesburg was in town Sunday.
B. V. Minton of Elk City was in town Tues.
B. V. Minton of Elk City was in town Tues.
H. B. Kelly of Kansas City was in town Tuesday.
D. S. Collard of Mo. was in town Tues.
J. A. Henley of Lawrence was in Tues.
J. I. David of Gro Isle, Michigan was in town Sunday.
A. L. Martin of Agency was in town Sun.
J. E. Dodson of Osage Territory was in town Tues.
I.A. Millepaugh of St. Joseph Mo was in town Tues.
Homer J. Hendricks of St Louis in town Tues.
The Mineral Springs Bath House has an ad in this issue.

Charles Vaughn made a trip to Indy Mon.

Theo Lockwood of Indy was in town Tuesday

C. C. Pershall returned home from last Tues.

J. E. Baker went to Sedan last Monday

W. A. Price of Peru was in on legal business.

Miss Anna Beatty of Havana is in the city visiting Dortha Slater.

George Vaughn went to Independence Mon.

Persimmons are getting ripe. Do not practice on green ones for they draw you like frothy.

Mrs. Rains has removed her millinery stock into the Baker's building.

The ball game between the independence and Sean clubs takes place today at the //independence ball ground.

Hi Woodring the grain buyer and Frank Cross the Implement and Hardware man are making our city their headquarters of late.

Mrs. C.W. Vaughn stated last monday to visit friends and relatives   at Eureka, Kansas. She will probably   be gone about a couple of weeks.

Mrs. Baker who has been attending the bedside of her sister at Fayetteville, Arkansas for some weeks past, returned home last Sunday evening.

We are in receipt of program of the Chautauqua County Teacher's Ass. To be held at Cedar Vale Nov. 3, 1888 commencing at 10 O'clock a.m.

Will Franks , Nic Kaufman, and number of others whose names we did not learn went to the nation on a hunting tour. They will probably be gone a couple of weeks.

F. Leatherock, S. M. Pearson, and Mr. Campbell of Cherryvale who have been in the nation hunting   passed through the city on their way home.

Oct. 19, 1888

Preparing for winter in order.
The social season is upon us.
Snow storms in the northern states.
A little fire feels good these cool days.
The crop in Kansas this year is the largest on record.
Farmers ought to be happy now that wheat is $1.00 per bushel.
House cleaning time has put in it's appearance and the stoves
have to be put up.
This is a favorable time to lay in a winter's supply of coal
provided you are able to pay for it.
Kansas is a great state but with sugar works springing up all
around she is destined to be much greater.
Only they who really work can fully appreciate what a blessing it
is to have one days rest out of the 7 days in the week.
The hunter is happy now. Game is so plentiful that they do not
have to tramp all day to get a good mess of Quail or chicken.
It must be very embarrassing for a young gentleman to be out
riding with a nice young lady and have the misfortune to become
minus the ---of his pants while gathering persimmons.

Local Happenings   10-19-1888

Everybody busy.—This is most like winter. Several deaths this
week. Pleasant day Wednesday—Persimmons are delicious--
/have you got up that heater? Quite windy for a few days past.
Sunday was a bad drizzled day. Lew Lynn went to Peru Wed.
Numerous strangers in town this week.—The leaves have changed
their color.—Soon the winter blast will be upon us.—our schools
are progressing very nicely.—Wheat is selling at $1.10 a bushel in
Cherryvale.—A large drove of hogs on the street Tuesday.—
Everything is quiet and peace reigns supreme.—
James Monroe is on the sick list this week.—One of Imel's little
girls is on the sick list.-Get down that overcoat and shape it up for
use.—John McFall of St. Louis was in town Monday—Same
Maples of Peru was in town Monday.—Susie Royce of Sedan was
in the city Sat.—I. G. Cotton of Sedan was in town last Sat.—R. J.

Williams of Evert, Mo. was in town Mon.—E. B. Strickland of St. Joe, Mo. was in town Sat. –F. G. Cross and lady of Elk City were in town Frid. Last—Prepare for winter and do not let it catch you unprepared.—Frank Peterson of Marshell, Mo. was in town last Sat.

It is after dark now and days when the passenger train arrives. Just see those elegant window shades at the furniture store.==J.W. Sipple went down to Independence last Frid. night to see the ball game and transact other business. Charley Vaughn thinks batching is not funny as it might be.—a number of Osage were up from the Territory the first of the week.—Hi Woodring the rustling grain buyer is perambulating our streets.—Mrs. Fritch is again able to be up, a fact that we are glad to mention. Several of our citizens are preparing for a big hunt inthe territory soon. George Vaughn called in Wed. and has us print him some note heads. Joe Fritch is looking rather bad as though he had undergone a severe spell of sickness.—Travel on the Rail Road is on the increase, the result of good crops in Kansas this year. Robert Harshbarger took quite a drive down into the territory last Monday.—Times are close and people are complaining .Come brace up and try to make things more lively. Hhere have been more deaths in and around the springs this fall then there have been for several years.---The candates have only a short time in which they will be held in suspence.The 6th. of Nov. settles it!------- Mr. Hilton is up from the Nation and informs us that he will immediatly open up a photograph gallerey here. C. E. Dunmore went down to Independence last Frid. And it is useless to say that he took in the ballgame.—The finest window shades ever put on the market are now for sale at T. J. Johnson's furniture store. Drop in and see them. The mill is again in good running order and it's buz' can be heard all hours of the day.==The Ball Game in Independence between Sedan and Independence clubs resulted in a score of 11-13 against the Sedan boys.—Reverand Alldredge preached his farewell sermon last Sunday evening to the people of Chautauqua Springs. When he goes from here we are unable to say "You ought to go down and look through the bath house since John Johnson has taken charge of it. Every thing neat and clean and baths given on short notice .—

J. C. Blair OF Havana was in the city Monday and made us a pleasant call. ..—Mrs. Blair is selling books containing the life of Harrison and Morton, and Cleveland, and Thurman.—I have a number of fine young cedar and Walnut trees which I am offering for sale cheap. I also have a number of kinds. Call at my farm 3 miles West of Chautauqua. Henry Sargent Died-Timble,-Tues. Oct. 16, infant child of Mr. and Mrs. Timble.—Higgin bottom Tuesday Oct. 16, infant child of Mr. and Mrs.   Higgin bottom of this city.

Wanted – I want 50 head of mules and ponies to winter on rough feed. For further info apply to the undersigned at his farm 3 miles of this city on E. side of Cedar Creek.==Henry Sargent

Sam Jones the sensational revivalist has made over $100,000.00 by his original style of saving sinners.   Miss

Mabel Chesney, daughter of respectable parents of Paulding Ohio has eloped with a negro who worked for her father. It is positively asserted that the young lady   near Kansas City who cleared $30,000.00 on wheat had 36 proposals in as many hours. ==The hen that cackles the loudest is not always the one that lays the biggest egg and the man who boasts most is not always the man of solid worth. The world will find out what you are without telling it yourself.

Oct. 26, 1888

Dir- City of Chautauqua, Chautauqua County
ME Church Rev. W. S. Browning
Union Sunday School Rev. C. W. Alldredge
Chautauqua G. A. R. 218   J. W. Sipple
Friends Lodge 285 100F

Rail Road Times Table

Western Rail Road
Western   Eastern
                    Add Local
This fall is earnest. –Cool is pleasant.—Autumn tints show up. Potatoes getting warmer.—Get in those broken glass.— The schools are doing well.—Persimmons being harvested .— Election day will soon be here.---New native sorghum in market.--

Thanks for the stupidity of the flies.—Politicians are becoming very anxious.—The man with the big pile of coal and plenty of wood is comparatively happy just now.—Eating caraway seed said not only to aid weak digestion but to make the eyes bright and strengthen the sight.—Corn is king this year. It has been 4 years since we have had such a corn crop.—There are millions in it. The baby Farmer Wm. Beattie who lives on the Cimarron River north of the Indian Territory line was carried off by an Eagle.=The council of the Sioux at the lower Brule Agency has dissolved and delegates from each of the 6 agencies. Will visit Washington.

Chautauqua House   J. C. Romick
T. J. Dunn and Son   Physician and Surgeon
T. J. Johnson—Furniture and Undertaker
J. N. Goff   Harness and saddles

Moody , the Evangelist is 51 and his mother is still living at an at an extremely advanced age. They reside at North field, Mass.
A Mrs. Manning of Paris, Ill. who died a few days since took to her bed 9 years ago declaring she would never leave it till she died because her son married a girl she did not like and she kept her word.
The men who took part in the female prize fight near Buffalo, New York are to be severely punished. Four have been convicted. The penalty is one years imprisonment or $500.00 fine.

Robert J. Burdett, the humorist has been licensed to preach the gospel. It is said that he intends to retire at once from the field of literature and lecturing and seek a change.

The cotton crop of 1888 is the largest ever grown in America exceeding that 1882-3. Hitherto the largest on record by 96000 bales. The total crop   this season 7,046,833 bales.

Oct 26, 1888 Local happings
The highest market price paid in cash for eggs and butter and drakes located in Bennets building.

Mr. Hilton is on the sick list this week.

Charles Rodd of Pawhuska was in the city Sat.

Notice the change in R.R. time table this week.

Don't forget the auction Sale tommow at 2:00.

H. B. Kelley of Kansas City was in Wed.

E. Townsend of Pawhuska was in the city Sat. last.

C. A. Clotfelter of Cherryvale was in the city Thursday.

Glen Thornton of Salina City, Mo.

We turned out some work for President Miller this week.

We printed a lot of posters for P.E. last week for Howard.

Miss Mamie Sawyer left Wed. for New Salem.

The 6th. of November draws near and anxious candidate waits his fate.

A new bank has opened in Sedan known as the Sedan State Bank.

George Edwards returned fromthe Nation Mon. evening with two fine deer.

Mrs. Robert L. Wells of Coffeyville is visiting with Mrs. Romick this week.

A brother of our agent Vawter has been visiting in this city for two weeks past.

Mrs. Rimick and children returned Tuesday evening from a visit at Coffeyville.

M. P. Freligh, detective for the Santa Fe railway waas in the city last week.

Remember the big sale one fourth mile South of Jonesburg on /Nov.. 1, 1888

C. A. McBrian of Sedan of Sedan was in the city last Sat. and made a pleasant call.

George Vaughn went to Independence Tues. thence to Cherryvale and Elk City.

Mrs. C. W. Vaughn returned home last Sat. eve after 2 weeks visit at Eurika with friend and relatives .

We printed some sale bills for F. E. Hendrix who lives near Jonesburg   Sat.

Ed Oliver visited his sister Mrs. J. E. Baker.J. E. Baker has been improving the kitchen on the rear of the hotel this week preparatory for winter .

Coffeyville is all excitement since the terrible explosion which occurred at that places Thursday of last week.

We printed Soper and Stallard a lot of posters last Friday for a big auction Sale tomorrow.

P. H. Howard has purchased the Post Office building of Jacob Kaufman and will soon remove his meat market into it.

R.W.M. Roe Republican candidate for state Senator will speak at the school house tomorrow evening at 7:30 o'clock.

Jim Butler and L.G. Soper were up from Chautauqua Springs last Monday shaking hands with old friends –Cherryvale Champion.

Oct. 26, 1888   Book 4

Col. David of Detroit Michigan was a long time U.S. Indian Agent of Pawhuska, I. T. is stopping at the Chautauqua House.

George W. Thrasher, the
Havana liveryman was in the city last Sat. and made us a pleasent call. He tells us that Havana is prospering and that he is enjoying a good business.

The Cherryvale Bullion is a good local paper and now H. M. Steward is editor and publisher he is having leased the offiice from Mr. Berry. We wish Bro Stewart success in his undertaking.

Mrs. Romick has a variety of ferns and mosses which she gathered near the spring. They are beautiful and if they can be made to grow after having been transplanted they will become very popular.

Nov. 2, 1888.   book 4

Pecans are plentiful.—4 days until election. This is fine fall weather. The cider continues to flow—The political pot boils furiously. Soon the politician will cease to roam.

Wheat fields are looking green and thrifty.—The festive little fly will soon be hunting winter quarters .—A new democrat paper has made it's appearance in Coffeyville. The ice man's occupation has ceased .—Jack Frost cut himself off.—Parents should see that these children are in school and not in the streets.—Republican speaking at the school house last Saturday night. By R. W. M. recorder. Several parties from this city and vicinity are down in the nation on a hunting expedition.—Live business men is what makes a live newspaper and the two combined makes a live town. A Vassar girl being asked by her teacher what kind of a noun it was both proper and common. The Governor of Kansas has offered a reward of $500.00 for the arrest and conviction of the scamp who left a box of dynamite at the express office at Coffeyville recently.—Altogether there is a reward of $1, 700.00 offered for the friend of the person who set the dynamite.

Local Happenings:
Lew Lynn went over to Sedan last Wed.
B. F. Ramey went to Sedan last Wed.
W. A. Price of Peru was in the city Tues.
Andrew McGuire has been quite sick this week.
Mike Foley of Osage Agency was in town Mon.
D. J. Moore of Sedan was in town Sat.
H. N. Coffin of Topeka was in town last Sat.
G. F. King of Parsons was in the city Monday.
G. A. Lawrence of Cedar Vale was in town Monday.
W. F. Rodimel of Sedan was in the city Monday.
S. H, Wilson of Cherryvale was in the city Monday.
Charles Fagan of Osage Agency was in town Monday.
Frank B. Williams of Pawhuska was in town Sat.
We printed George Edwards a lot of letter head notes this week.
Mr. Fairbanks has moved into north part of this city.
For Sale- A good coal stove. Inquire of A. C. Cadwell.
J. M. Gravely of Independence was in city Sat.
Long Bell Lumber Company received another car of coal.
Rev. Browning moved his family into the parsonage last Wed.
Henry Fisher of Cedar Vale was perambulating on streets Monday.
Mart Drake was over at Coffeyville the first of the week on business.
C. A. Clotfelter was down from Cherryvale again Mon. on business.
Mr. Hilton is still on sick list with little improvement in his condition.
William Charles, road master on the Rail Road was in the city Sat.

Still the dynamite explosion is being discussed by the different papers all over the state.

Born-Thursday night Oct. 25th to Mr. and Mrs. George S. Vaughn, an 8 pd. Boy.

P. R. Rains has returned from the Territory where he has been for several months.

K. H. Malone called Monday and ordered the Express sent to a friend.

Mrs. R. L. Wells who has been visiting with Mrs. Romick returned to her home in Coffeyville last month.

A. J. Miller of the firm of Forsyth and Miller, Attorney at law of Winfield was a pleasant caller this last week.

Some parties went serenading last Mon. night after the democrat Speaking and kept it up until nearly daylight Tuesday morning.

A. Y. Buckles od Sedan was in town last Tuesday lucking up his chances for reelection to this office of Co Superintendent.

Avery Pershall still walks with crutches from the effect of an accidental discharge of a Winchester, the ball taking effect in the right foot.

Mrs. Ike Imel and children and Miss Dortha Slater went up to Elk City last Sat. to visit friends and relatives. Mr. Imel went up after them last week.

Mrs. Soper, wife of our general shoe maker and facility of Cherryvale arrived in the city last Sunday evening and now reside in the building just east of the Chautauqua House.

J. E. Baker, Lew Lynn, J. L. Stallard, George L. Dunn, Charles E. Dunmore,L. J. Soper, Alonzza Vancil, Charles H. Vaughn and James Ferguson went to Sedan last Friday to a big Republican speaking.

We are in receipt of Volume 1, No. 2of the Kansas News published at Topeka by the News Publishing Co. with C. E. Prather as Editor. The News and a neat column sheet published monthly.

Nov. 9, 1888

Additional Local:
Election is over—Beautiful.
Weather- The agony is over.
Considerable confusion in town —election day.

Wild geese are on the wing, their course is toward the South. Now is the times to examine your chimney and flues and have them cleaned.

The next legal holiday is Thanksgiving Day. Now commence to fatten the turkey.

The fellow whose bets we won on the wrong side wish now that he hadn't since election day.

A. L. Wilson has sold his interest in the Cherryvale Republican to Col. C. P. Buffington, formally of The Globe and Torch of the city. The Col' is a good newspaper man and if there is any success in the newspaper business he is the man to bring it about.

Local Happenings: Rather cool . Beautiful snow.—Winter is close at hand.—Heating stoves are in demand.—Mrs. Hilton is able to be up and around again. –Dan M. Pile od Sedan was in the city Monday.—Billy Robison of Sedan was in town Monday.—J. C. Blair of Havana was in the city last Wed.—H, B. Kelly of Kansas City was in the city Thurs. –B. V. Minton of Elk City was in the city last Thurs.—Considerable money changes hands on this election in the city.—P. M. Doyle of Osage Agency was in the city Saturday. A fair fax spoke at all the school house Monday.— The streets are in a very slushy, wet, and disagreeable condition. H. J. Hendrick and wife of Cedar Vale were in the city last Thursday. –William Rains has severed his connection with The Elephant Livery Stable.—J. W. Sipple returned from his hunting trip in the Nation Wed.—Some are sore over the election while others are jubilant, for such is the way of the world.—We printed T. J. Dunn a lot of sale bills this week. The sale will be held Sat. November 17th. J. T. Pershall and several others will go to the nation in the near future on an extended hunting expedition.—I have an unlimited amount wood which I will sell cheap. I will sell in almost ant shape a man wants—Henry Sergeant.—J. D. Brian and son and Mrs. Deshazo of Sedan passed through the city last Wed. enrout to the Nation where they will spend a few days hunting.—Dr. J. W. Myers, the gentleman from Ark City who has purchased Barretts stock of drugs was a pleasant caller last Wed. and ordered an add in the Express and also had us enroll his name on our subscription list. The doctor came well recommended and is permanently located with us. Success to him.

Nation News

Dr. Kennedy has had his house enlarged and recovered on his Sand Creek place and now has plenty of roon. By the way the doctor is a good marksman and has killed 5 prairie chickens at one shot. –Quite a number of Osages are camped on Sand Creek, at first house below Felix's during their accustomed feast. John Papan was up doing some trading at the Springs last week. John is one of the steady men of the Nation. –Heavy prairie fires in the Nation near Rock Creek.—The whole face of the country was one vast sheet of flames Monday night last. ---

Dr. J. W. Myers –Physician and Surgeon.-
Office in Barrett's Building—Chautauqua, Ks.

Purcell and Beaston---Real Estate and Exchange Agents

Jacob Kaufman—Confectionary, stock, candies, nuts, oydters, Crackers, lemons, oranges, cidar, cigars, tobbacco, country produce bought and sold.

J.E. Baker   Commercial Hotel $1.00 per day. First Class- Good Clean Beds and Rooms, and Table furnished with the best the Market can afford.

November 16 , 1888

Christmas in six weeks—Get a new Almanacs for 1899 are out. Old 1888 is on it's last quarter.—Wild geese are hunting a warmer climate.—Thanksgivings day on the 29th.—
Wheat growing right along and looking well.—Long winter evenings are gradually advancing upon us.—Some men are like rives-small heads and big mouths, - President Cleveland has issued his thanks—proclamation—It is predicted that the approaching winter will be severe and the turkeys has passed a resolution to roost a limb or two higher.—See that all cellars and basements are cleaned out and purified before the winter season. Typhoid fever and other malarial diseases may this be avoided.—

The citizens of Western Kansas who have the grit to hold out a few years longer will wake up some fine morning to reap the full rewards of their fortitude.

Local Happenings

Holiday goods coming in.
D. Severns of Peru was in town Sunday.
Remember the big stock sale tomorrow.
E. C. Hill of Peru was in town last Tuesday.
Charles Dunmore is on the sick list this week.
j. A. Blackburn of Sedan was in town Sunday
Read F. H. Hawkins new ad.
Allen Cook of Pawn Creek was in town Sunday.
John Buckles of Peru was in town Sunday.
Dr. J. D. Stevens of Peru was in town Mon.
Howard is selling fresh bread at his meat market.
R. J. Hill of Independence was in town Monday.
Ed Oliver went down to Independence Mon.
C. A. Clotfelter of Cherryvale was in the city .
Charles Vaughn was on the sick list the first of the week.
G. A. Gentry of Salina, Ks. Was in town Monday.
George Edwards is enjoying the hunt in the Nation this week.
Mr. and Mrs. Emens of Sedan were in the city Sun.
Sam Maples of Peru was in town 1st. of week
J. E. Baker went down to the Territory Wed. am
Mr. Deshazo and son of Sedan were in the city Wed.
F. E. Hendrix of Jonesburg called Wed.
Milla Breeding of East Lynn, Mo. was in city Wed.
Leonard Revard of Pawhuska   was in town Wed.
F. H. Hawkins left   us an order for a lot of letter heads.
Mrs. Rain has had the interior of her Millinery room repaired.
J. T. Pershall is down in the Territory this week on a hunting expedition.
George S. Hartley and wife of Pawhuska were in town Wed.
Several full bloods were up from the nation this week doing some trading.
The Post Office was removed into the red front building last Tuesday am.

Mr. Hilton and family have moved into the building just west of the Lumber Yard.

Lew Lynn has been granted a pension of $8.00 per month, a fact we are glad to mention.

Will Lane is running the barber shop while the proprietor is recovering from his illness.

P. R. Howard has put a partition in his building which adds much to it's appearance inside.

Have your flues and stove pipes cleaned and arranged so that there is no danger of fire breaking out.

The Caney Chronicle has changed hands, a gentleman from Fredonia having purchased the out fit from Mr. McFee.

Will Scott the jovial good natured traveling salesman for Paul's Grocery of Independence who has been laid up for a month past with erysipelas was in the city last month.

James Teter of Pryor Creek, Osage Nation was visiting with J. H. Fairley and family and other old friends last week and transacting some legal business. Mr. Teter was one of the first settlers on Big Cana in 1871 and regards the old settlers as almost as dear to him as brothers. He returned home the tenth,

November 23. 1888

Add Local:

News might be scarce.—Stock water is plenty.—Lots of strangers in town.—A hard winter is predicted. Wild geese are on the wing.—Look up your winter wraps.—Penned porkers are fattening.—The turkeys are roosting high.—Leap year is on the home stretch.—Winter wheat is up and looks fine.—The byways are strewn with dead leaves.—The campaign liar is now resting his face.—Already predictions for 1890 are being made.—The prettiest things in fall bonnets are the faces.---The man who was elected to a fat office is happy.—Don't forget it, every dollar spent at home is a help to our local prosperity.—If you owe the printer pay him.—Money would come in mighty handy these days.— There is an atmosphere of funeral gloom hanging over the post office in Kansas. –Kansas built this year to Nov. 1, four hundred and seventy six miles of rail road, 476 miles.

Local Happenings:

Coal is somewhat scarce. 1 more issue in this month .
Lew Lynn went to Sedan.
The Joe Fritch is learning to be a Post Master.
W. Lewis of Osage was in town Sun.
Reverand Browning is a little under the weather.
R. C. Johnson has several head of horses missing.
Paul Aiken of Pawhuska was in town Monday.
C. A. McBrian of Sedan was in town Wed.
Jake Kaufman went down to the Agency yesterday.
Mart Drake was down to Coffeyville Sat.
Miss Ella Morgan of Elgin was in the city Tues.
John Terry of Kansas City Wed.
C. A. Senor of Osage Agency was in town Sun.
J. McLaughlia of Osage was in town Sunday
S. H. Hamilton of Kansas City were in town Wed.
G. H. Snow of Fall City Neb. was in town Sunday.
Charles Brown of Osage Nation was in town Tues.
We printed Randall and Oliver a lot of bill heads this week.
H. G. Coziluis of Kansas City was in the city Wed.
J. N. Goff gave us an order for letter heads and statements this week.
W. A. Franks, our genial lumber man went over to Sedan Wed.
Charles Fagan was up from Agency last Sat. attending some business.
Robert Wright, brother of the editor,of Elk City is learning the printers trade with us.
George Thrasher , the livery man of Havana was in the city Wed. and failed not to call at our office.
George H. Williams, brother and Kitty V. Williams niece, Mrs. J. C. Romick came down from Independence Tues. and returned Thursday.
T. J. Johnson, our undertaker was at Peru one day last week and purchased the undertakers stock of goods, thus there is but one establishment of the kind in township.
George Edwards and J. T. Pershall returned home Mon. from their extended hunting trip with a number off turkeys and other small game but without killing a deer.

Jonesburgh is busted. The only general store will be removed to our city the first of the coming week. Her only drug store is being packed for removal to our thriving and prosperous. Little city and in all probabilities the black smith shop will also be removed into our city leaving Jonesburgh without a business enterprise of any kind. Score another for our city—the most progressive of any in Southern Kansas. The demand for business and residence houses is still increasing and we do not know of a vacant house in the city.

Every person has two educations –one which he receives from others and one, more important which he gives himself.

Add local   Nov. 30,1888

Lots of hogs and cattle are being fed around the place.
Take care of your farm and garden machinery and tools.
The poor cotton tails are having a rough time of it now.
Some of the 1889 calendars are very unique and attractive.
Now work up the business booming.
Talking politics is now only a waste of time.
Christmas will soon be here---1888 will soon be gone and another year ended almost.---The little folks are already beginning to count the days between now and Christmas.—Five country dailies in Kansas have succumbed to the inevitable sence, the election. No man ever did a designed injury to another without doing a greater to himself. Douglas County this year produced an apple 18 inches in circumferences and weighing 3 pounds. This is not a campaign lie.

Joe Johnson – dealer in furniture, Burial Robes, Caskets, Coffins, Burial Slippers and everything in undertakers line.
Chairs, Sofas, Stands, Bedsteads, Tables

Our merchants have been doing a good business every day since the election.
Joe Fritch is now an Attorney having been admitted to the bar last month.

T. J. Johnson sent a coffin up to Peru last Monday but we did not learn who it was for.

Ethel Romick went to Coffeyville Thur. morning to spend Thanksgiving with Mrs. Wells and family.

The Elk City Eagle while soaring around recently was surprised to discover the remains of the Fredonia Chronicle.

Jacob Kaufman has traded for a stock of shelf hardware which he is opening up this week.

Our farmers have about all quit talking politicks and are devoting their tremendous corn crop,

A gentleman named Davis had one of his toes amputated last month. From the effect of having cut it with an ax some time ago.

Miss Eva Guthery of Wauneta, sister of Mrs. J.W. Myers is visiting.

Mrs. J. W. Myers is visiting in the city this week and will probably remain in the city this week.

Died: Peter Revard died at his home in the Indian Territory last Sat.

Died: David Wilson died at his home near Elgin, Kansas, on Sat. last.

The Chautauqua House has been doing a good business the PAST WEEK. Following are a number of arrivals:

J. R. Anstram of	Fort Scott
Thos. Leaky of	Elgin
John J. Ryan of	Mc Pherson
E. Garnett of	Wichita
W. S. Mathews of	IT
John McFall and daughter of	St. Louis
R. A. Long of	Columbus
Henry T. McNutt of	St Joe, Mo.
W. C. Tucker of	Sedalia, Mo.
R. E. Dodson of	Pawhuska
Ed H. Wheeler of	Kansas City
D. E. Wassam of	Independence
Miss Miller of	Pawhuska
J. M. Rogers, Jas Wood	
John Garman	Wichita
J. T. Shearman---	Wichita
W. I. Shepard	Wichita
B. B. Cushman	Wichita
Henry Huff	Buffalo, N. Y.
Allen Cook -	Osage Agency
John Baker—	Pearl, Ill.
B. V. Minton –	Elk City
John Baker	Pearl, Ill.
Allen Cook	Osage Agency

Dec.7, 1888

Add Local:

Cranberry sauce.—Hunters are active.—
It will soon be 1889.—Worry kills more men than work
The sharper gets rich off his credulous victims.
Some of the alleys are not in the best condition.

It is said cider will cure Rheumatism.—A cheap remedy

Honey is said to be a remedy for insomnia.
It should be eaten freely on bread before retiring.

How a woman can keep talking while she twists her hair back
with half a dozen hair pens in her mouth is a mystery, yet not
explained.

Kansas in five years will make her own sugar and in ten years will
have millions of pounds to sell. This is not slow for the

SUNFLOWER STATE.

Wonder if our young ladies will have any Leap Year parties
before the year closes. Remember girls, only a little less than one
month remains.

Reports continue to come from all over Southern Kansas showing
that the yield of all crops and the total produced of the farms have
never been so GREAT!

12-7-1888

Auction Sale tomorrow.
Mrs. Ike Imel is on the sick list.
J. Blenn of New York was in town last Monday.
Lew Lynn had us print him some letter heads.
Charles Vaughn went down ti Independence last Mondat.
M. D. Hampton of Osage was in town last Monday.
We printed J.W. Harshbarger and Co. some posters this week.
J. H. Beatty of Johnesburg was over Sat. on business.
Rev. J. R. Robinson was a pleasant caller at this place Monday.
B. F. Adams of Sedan was in town on business.
Miss Florence Guthrie is now staying with Mrs. George Vaughn.
F. N. Bostwick of Cleveland, Ohio was in the city last week.
W. G. Rogers of Jonesburg was in our little city last Sat.
Samuel Mc Gee of Elgin was in town Mon.
J. B. Ziegler of Independence in our town Monday.
 The corn stalks are not killing cattle this year. Stalk fields have a great value for feed.
C. A. Clotfelter of Cherryvale was in city Monday.
Dr. J. W. Myers visited his father in town.
Mrs. Randall returned last Tues. evening from two weeks visit at Fayetteville, Arkansas.
George Guthers at Wauneta
Dr. B. D. Brown and lady of Havana city were in city last Monday as guests of Ike Imel and family.
Mrs. George Vaughn returned last Monday evening after visit with friends and relatives in Eureka.
The long looked for car of coal arrived Monday night and Tuesday it was distributed among our citizens. This is the season when a boy will walk 15 miles following a rabbit tract but when told to bring in a hod of coal has pain in every joint.
Alfred Soper, son of our genial shoe maker come in from California last Friday. We had the misfortune to get his to get his right hand seriously mashed while coupling cars on the RR recently.
Married! Richardson – Hodges   by Justice of the peace Lew Lynn

At his office Nov. 29th. Mr. Isaac Richardson to
Mrs. Nancy Hodges. Of Hewins, Kansas.   Next Dec. 14, 1888.

The beautiful Chautauqua Springs are still a beautiful Place to visit.

The Chautauqua Springs are still running out pure crystal clear water

The running water is cold and clear.

**The beautiful sand rocks and ferns still grace
the flowing water**

The many trees and ferns always gives off
The freshest smells

Kansas is basis of the film Wizard of Oz

Teddy Roosevelt came and took baths in these
Healing water surrounded by all this beauty.

Come and check it out!

**Enjoy these Chautauqua Springs
with us**

Visit us soon

Made in the USA
Columbia, SC
30 October 2018